W9-BZC-015

Reading and Interpreting the Works of

TONI
MORRISON

Enslow Publishing
101 W. 23rd Street
Suite 240
New York, NY 10011
USA
enslow.com

Lit Crit Guides

Reading and Interpreting the Works of

Lisa A. Crayton

TONI MORRISON

*To my son, Josiah Antonio Herrera. Thanks for the joy,
laughter and love you add to my life!*

Published in 2016 by Enslow Publishing, LLC
101 W. 23rd Street, Suite 240, New York, NY 10011

Library of Congress Cataloging-in-Publication Data
Crayton, Lisa A.
 Reading and interpreting the works of Toni Morrison / Lisa A. Crayton.
   pages cm. — (Lit crit guides)
 Includes bibliographical references and index.
 Summary: "Describes the life and work of author Toni Morrison"— Provided by publisher.
 ISBN 978-0-7660-7352-4
1. Morrison, Toni—Juvenile literature. 2. Morrison, Toni—Criticism and interpretation. 3. Nov-
elists, American—20th century—Biography—Juvenile literature. 4. African American novelists,
American—20th century—Biography—Juvenile literature. I. Title.
 PS3563.O8749Z6128 2016
 813'.54—dc23
 [B]
                              2015028589
Printed in the United States of America

To Our Readers: We have done our best to make sure all website addresses in this book were active
and appropriate when we went to press. However, the author and the publisher have no control over
and assume no liability for the material available on those websites or on any websites they may link
to. Any comments or suggestions can be sent by e-mail to customerservice@enslow.com.

Portions of this book originally appeared in *A Student's Guide to Toni Morrison*.

Photo Credits: Cover, Timothy Greenfield-Sanders; p. 3 PASCAL GUYOT/AFP/Getty Images; p. 6
Francois Durand/Getty Images Entertainment/Getty Images; p. 8 Alex Wong/Getty Images News/
Getty Images; p. 12 Transcendental Graphics/Archive Photos/Getty Images; p. 16 Hulton Archive/
Getty Images; p 22 James Keyser/The LIFE Images Collection/Getty Images; pp. 28, 96, 116 © AP
Images; p. 40 Alfred Eisenstaedt/The LIFE Picture Collection/Getty Images; p. 43 Archive Photos/
Getty Images; pp. 49, 104 Hulton Archive/Getty Images; pp. 54, 60 Popperfoto/Getty Images; p.
72 Bohbeh/Shutterstock.com; p. 78 PATRICK KOVARIK/AFP/Getty Images; p. 84 Declan Huan/
Shicago History Museum/Archive Photos/Getty Images; p. 91 Ann Ronan Pictures/Print Collector/
Hulton Archive/Getty Images; p. 99 Library of Congress, Prints and Photographs Division; p. 109
Charles H. Phillips/The LIFE Picture Collection/Getty Images; p. 121 Marion Curtis/DMI/The LIFE
Picture Collection/Getty Images; p. 125 Bobby Bank/WireImage/Getty Images; p. 127 Scott Olson/
Getty Images News/Getty Images; p. 128 FRANCK FIFE/AFP/Getty Images.

CONTENTS

Chapter 1 Presidential Honor:

The Life and Career of Toni Morrison...... 7

Chapter 2 Pioneering Author: Major Themes......... 21

Chapter 3 Creative Genius:

Morrison's Background 37

Chapter 4 Reclaiming Racial

Beauty: *The Bluest Eye* 53

Chapter 5 Freedom Flight: *Song of Solomon* 77

Chapter 6 More Than a Ghost Tale: *Beloved* 94

Chapter 7 The Dancing Mind:

Toni Morrison Today.................... 120

Chronology 131

Chapter Notes 134

Literary Terms 145

Major Works by Toni Morrison 146

Further Reading 147

Websites 148

Index 149

Toni Morrison

1

PRESIDENTIAL HONOR: THE LIFE AND CAREER OF TONI MORRISON

Toni Morrison sat regally in the East Room of the White House. She applauded as other honorees received the Presidential Medal of Freedom that day, May 29, 2012. Then it was her turn. With President Barack Obama's help, she rose from her seat. She stepped forward to hear a citation about her works and contributions to society. During the presentation, she was called "one of our nation's most distinguished storytellers."[1]

> She has captivated readers through lyrical prose that depicts the complexities of a people and challenges our concepts of race and gender. Her works are hallmarks of the American literary tradition, and the United States proudly honors her for her nursing of souls and strengthening the character of our union.[2]

President Obama presented the award to the author. Morrison returned to her seat, having just received "the Nation's highest civilian honor, presented to individuals who have made especially meritorious contributions to the security or national interests of the United States, to world peace, or to cultural or other significant public or private endeavors."[3]

Morrison receives the Presidential Medal of Freedom from President Obama in 2012.

Magic Unleashed

Few authors ever stand before the president of their nation to receive an award from that country. It was forty-two years from the time Morrison published her first novel in 1970 to the day she received the award. Along the way, she became famous for penning fiction that stretched readers' imaginations. The *New York Times* featured Morrison in an article called "The Radical Vision of Toni Morrison." Rachel Kaadzi Ghansah wrote, "The perplexing but wonderful thing about Morrison's career is just how much her prominence was created not by the mainstream publishing world, but by Morrison herself, on her own terms, in spite of it."[4]

Imagine a world where the past and present mingle. Legends abound, and all things seem possible. People fly, trees talk, ghosts rise. Welcome to Toni Morrison's magical world of fiction. Ghosts, spirits, mythic characters, and magical events drift through her novels as the present suffuses with memories. Points of view change and blend. Conversations are slow and easy, punctuated with the lyrical vernacular (language) of the old South.[5]

Morrison is one of the world's most respected African-American novelists. She has received the Nobel Prize for Literature, the Pulitzer Prize, and many other awards. Her first book, *The Bluest Eye*, was published in 1970. It did not attract as much attention as Morrison had hoped. She kept writing anyway. Eventually her fame spread.

Morrison's memorable characters are one reason for her appeal. Readers and critics also praise her complex plots. Morrison writes about a variety of subjects and eras. *Beloved* is set during the era of slavery in America. *Jazz* is about the Harlem Renaissance. *Paradise* explores the 1970s. Morrison

CELEBRATING ARTS AND LITERATURE

There was a time when the eyes of the world focused on African-American creativity. Art and literature were especially celebrated. The era was called the Harlem Renaissance. It was birthed in the 1920s in Harlem, a neighborhood in New York City. During the mass migration of African Americans from the rural, agricultural South to the urban, industrial North (1914–1918), many who came to New York settled in Harlem.[6] They wanted jobs. They also wanted freedom from racism. It is estimated that more than 750,000 persons left the South during this time. Of that number, about 175,000 moved to Harlem.[7]

The area soon became a sophisticated literary and artistic center.[8] Writers and artists, many of whom lived in Harlem, began to produce a wide variety of fine and highly original works dealing with African-American life.[9] Soon more magazines, newspapers, and books were being published. Most of these magazines and newspapers did not survive.

Traditional publishers took notice. They wanted to release works by African Americans. Some of the nation's most celebrated writers and poets were first published at this time. These include Claude McKay, Arna Bontemps, James Weldon Johnson, and Langston Hughes. Zora Neale Hurston also began publishing during the Harlem Renaissance.

As the literary movement took off, so did a new musical form: jazz. Southern black musicians brought jazz with them to the North and to Harlem.[10] It is still popular today.

The era faded with the Great Depression. The country's troubles made it hard to focus on artistic expression. As it died down, interest in works by African Americans died down somewhat. Harlem's fame also slipped, but today it remains a center of African-American culture and business.

considers the three books as a series. Her works show her interest in historical topics. She says, "I'm interested in the way in which the past affects the present and I think that if we understand a good deal more about history, we automatically understand a great more about contemporary life. Also, there's more of the past for imaginative purposes than there is of the future."[11]

Morrison is not afraid to address complex issues. She does not let us off easy, for each of Toni Morrison's novels contains brutal facts of inhumanity and injustice.[12] Morrison explains, "I'm just trying to look at something without blinking, to see what it is like, or it could have been like, and how that had something to do with the way we live now. Novels are always inquiries for me."[13]

Relevant Subjects

Morrison employs six major themes in her works. They are race relations, community and cultural issues, personal identity, relationships, spirituality, and sexuality. She weaves these themes into most of her fiction. She does not sugarcoat them to appeal to readers. Her stories of individualized pain and triumph resonate within the larger African-American experience.[14]

Most-Used Literary Techniques

The most common literary devices used by Morrison are irony, symbolism, ambiguity, and call-and-response.

Irony is a literary device that conveys the opposite meaning rather than the literal, or actual, meaning of a concept. In *Beloved*, Sweet Home appears to be a special kind of plantation. The plantation's name and original operations appear harmless. Some slaves buy into the image. They believe the

The Harlem Renaissance was an exciting time for African-American writers as well as other artists, like jazz musician Louis Armstrong, seen here with his band.

plantation is a cozy place to live. They do not realize their mistake until a new master arrives. He steps in and reinforces the plantation's role as a place of bondage. Morrison's use of irony is underscored by Paul D. He tells Denver that Sweet Home "wasn't sweet and it sure wasn't home." The meaning of the plantation's name contradicts the condition of slavery. Such contradiction highlights the problems slaves faced.

Morrison ties irony to symbolism when she uses Sweet Home as the name for the plantation. Symbolism is a literary device that allows a person or thing to represent someone or something else. In Morrison's novels, housing represents more than a place to live. The type and condition of an apartment or house provide a key to a character's income, personality, and relationships.

In *The Bluest Eye*, for example, the Breedloves live in a run-down apartment. It reflects the family's poverty. Later we learn it also symbolizes how family members view themselves. They feel ugly, so they live in an ugly house.

In Morrison's work, flying is a metaphor for several ideas. Perhaps the most important are freedom, abandonment, and control over one's destiny. When Shalimar flies home to Africa in *Song of Solomon*, he is free from all restrictions. He abandons his children and his wife, Ryna. She loses her mind from the grief of a broken heart.

Ambiguity is another common device of Morrison's. At the end of *Beloved*, the ghost-woman disappears. Morrison does not say why. This is an example of ambiguity in her novel. This device draws readers into a literary work. It allows them to take an event in the story or even the book's outcome and decide for themselves what actually took place.

Song of Solomon is another work that ends on an ambiguous note. After Guitar kills Pilate, Milkman turns to him.

"You want my life?" Milkman was not shouting now. "You need it? Here." Without wiping away the tears, taking a deep breath, or even bending his knees—he leaped. As fleet and bright as a lodestar he wheeled toward Guitar and it did not matter which one of them would give up his ghost in the killing arms of his brother. For now he knew what Shalimar knew: If you surrendered to the air, you could *ride* it.[15]

irony

A literary device that usually expresses the opposite, rather than the actual or literal meaning, of a word or phrase.

symbolism

A literary device that uses a person or thing to represent someone or something else.

Readers wonder about the ending. Did Milkman actually fly off Solomon's Leap? Did he commit suicide? Did he land safely and fight Guitar? Did one of them die? Morrison does not answer any of these questions. Readers must decide.

Morrison's novels also use call-and-response, which invites reader participation. Examples of call-and-response in *Beloved* include Baby Suggs's meetings in the Clearing and the community women's actions that free Sethe from *Beloved*.

Call-and-response actually originated in Africa as an oral storytelling device. As it developed further during slavery, call-and-response was a means for slaves to communicate with each other. Slaves were not allowed to talk with each other, but they could sing. Call-and-response evolved as a way for slaves to transmit important messages, especially those about upcoming escapes. Only the intended hearers could under-stand such messages. Hearers would sing their response.

Morrison shows how this worked in *Beloved*. Sweet Home slaves await a signal to escape. When it comes, the signal to run is transmitted in a song. The song means nothing to the slave owners, but it informs slaves of a pending escape.

Today, many African-American churches still use a form of call-and-response, with congregations having opportunities to respond at various times during a religious service.

The Author's Style

Versatility is the hallmark of Morrison's narrative style. Each novel is different. She adapts her style to suit the setting of each book.

One constant is Morrison's lyrical style. Her novels, at times, read like poetry or music. Barbara Hill Rigney explains that "Morrison also sings her work ... Images of music pervade her work, but so also does a musical quality of language, a sound and rhythm that permeate and radiate in every novel."[16] Morrison employs punctuation, dialogue, pacing, and other techniques to achieve lyricism.

metaphor
A literary device in which one thing is said to be another.

ambiguity
The quality of being obscure, in doubt, or uncertain.

The music in her works varies. Her novels include songs. She draws on gospel, Negro spirituals, jazz, the blues, and other types of music. Each of these musical forms has played an important role in African-American history. By including music, she shows its cultural meaning. Music serves as both a method of communication and entertainment for African Americans.

Morrison invokes the call-and-response practice of slaves in some of her work. The back-and-forth "conversations" in their songs often served as code for a planned escape. These slaves are standing outside their cabin in the mid-1800s.

One enjoyable example of her use of music is found in *The Bluest Eye*. Poland, one of the three prostitutes who befriends Pecola, sings,

> I know a boy who is sky-soft brown
> I know a boy who is sky-soft brown
> The dirt leaps for joy when his feet touch the ground
> His strut is a peacock
> His eye is burning brass
> His smile is sorghum syrup drippin' slow-sweet to the last
> I know a boy who is sky-soft brown.[17]

The imagery of this delightful song moves the novel along. So does the slave narrative in *Beloved*. It enhances the novel's historical flavor. A narrative offers a first-person account of events. It reads like a journal, or diary, entry.

Morrison switches to a third-person narrator in *The Bluest Eye*. She adds complexity to the work by having Claudia share her views both as a child and as an adult. The adult view adds balance, which helps readers better understand the flow of events.

The narrative style in *Jazz* is different still. It has an upbeat, musical style that makes the jazz era come alive for readers.

Indeed, Morrison's style stretches the imagination. However, it can be daunting. Readers not accustomed to an author style-switching may have difficulty following some of her fiction. It may help to keep an open mind while reading her works.

Heartfelt Language

Morrison does not rely on one language pattern. She changes language to create lifelike characters. She employs African-American speech, folklore, and mythology. Characters' language and thoughts reveal their backgrounds, providing clues to every area of their lives.

Holding nothing back, Morrison's characters freely express themselves. Language brings the novel's setting to life, be it a field, back porch, or posh resort. Readers can expect the unexpected—including slang and even profanity—as characters speak from their hearts.

Morrison utilizes language to show a character's change of heart. In *Song of Solomon*, Milkman hears of Hagar's death after he returns from his ancestral home. He is a changed man, with a better outlook on life. His language and attitude change to reflect this.

Morrison likes to add plot twists to her novels. Such twists add depth to her fiction. Readers who continue on to the end of each work, despite the complexity of the language and plot, will discover novels worth reading again and again.

Memorable Characters

Professor of African-American studies Barbara Christian notes:

> [At] first glance, each of [Morrison's] novels may seem to be primarily about one character: Pecola in *The Bluest Eye*, Sula in *Sula*, and Milkman Dead in *Song of Solomon*. But as we read the novels, what impresses us is not only these characters, but their blood relations. The people from whom the major characters derive their sense of themselves are as memorable, as finely drawn, as the focal characters.[18]

Morrison's protagonists are usually characters in transition, journeying through mysterious circumstances and personal histories to the innermost psyche, often to a triumphant discovery of selfhood.[19] People are as varied as the colors in a box of crayons or a painter's palette. They are young and old, rich and poor, sane and insane, good and evil, alive and dead. Morrison never clones her characters. They often struggle with some of the same issues but handle them in a variety of ways. Her body of work contains many contrasting characters.

In all Morrison's books, the particular concept that is foremost in her mind is divided into different aspects that her characters embody. In *The Bluest Eye*, the idea of physical beauty is examined in terms of its impact on black girls and women along class lines and skin shade. In *Sula*, the idea of woman is represented by the many female archetypes that the world has invented, from the domineering Eva through the handmaiden Nel to the witch Sula. In *Song of Solomon*, Morrison investigates the meaning of black racial identity, how the common history is responsible for people as diverse as the rebellious Guitar, the materialistic Macon, and the spiritual Pilate. And in *Tar Baby*, where the relationship between class and race is pivotal, Morrison introduces white characters, the wealthy Valerian and his wife, as well as non-American blacks, Gideon and Therese, who are practically serfs in their Caribbean home.[20] Morrison has a knack for creating complex, memorable characters. Achieving this is not easy. She explains, "The hard part is trying to make characters that aren't easily dismissed—sometimes, even people you admire—in other words, people that are just like us. My job is to make sure that my characters are people just like us. I don't know people that are less complicated than that."[21]

Critical Review

Critics have tried to label Morrison's work, but she escapes definition. Her writing does not neatly fit into any specific group. She can also write about multiple issues and eras. And she does it well, time and time again. Professor Trudier Harris contends, "Morrison succeeds in taking her readers into fantastic worlds where fantasy diminishes in direct proportion to our recognition of suffering humanity. She does not, she maintains, create characters who are larger than life; her conception of life is large enough to contain all of them."[22]

PIONEERING AUTHOR: MAJOR THEMES

Morrison began writing novels because she could not find the types of books she wanted to read. Biographer Stephanie Li explains:

> As Morrison has repeatedly stated, she wrote her first novel "in order to read it." This comment suggests that before committing pen to paper, she imagined herself as a reader, envisioning the books she wanted to read and the characters she wanted to know. Despite her prodigious study of literature, she was still hungry for books that described her experience and perspective as a black woman.[1]

"It is also true," according to journalist Rachel Kaadzi Ghansah, "that a sizeable portion of her audience simply looks like her, in a world where black Americans, and people of color in general, are still perceived to be nonreaders. But of course Morrison, rather than feeling marginalized or slighted by that criticism, takes delight in it."[2]

protagonist

The main character of a novel, drama, or other literary work.

For all of her readers, Morrison writes about real issues of life. She never offers easy answers, which readers appreciate. Her main themes—race relations, community/cultural issues, personal identity, relationships, spirituality, and sexuality—are often difficult and messy. Author Denise Heinze points out:

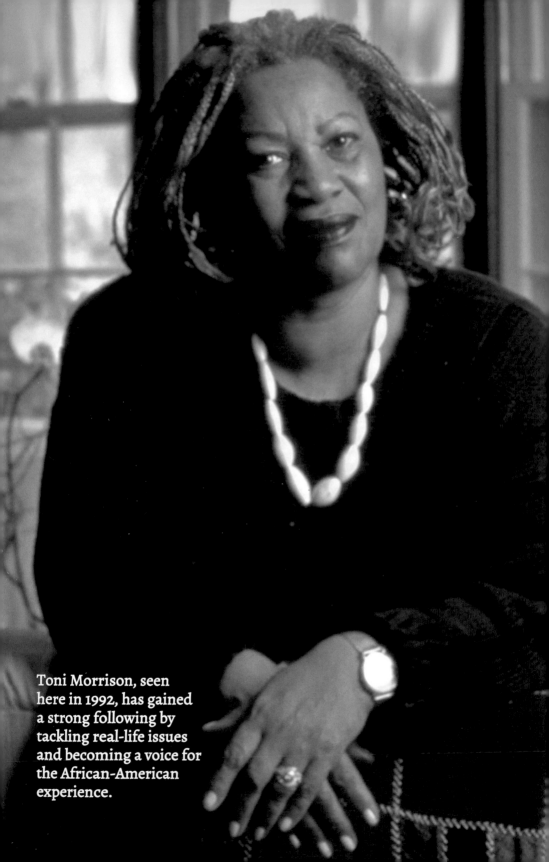

Toni Morrison, seen here in 1992, has gained a strong following by tackling real-life issues and becoming a voice for the African-American experience.

[S]he is a mythbasher in a country where writers have been canonized for creating and perpetuating the myths that form the foundation of the American way of thinking: the cult of domesticity and true womanhood, romantic love and ideal standards of beauty, capitalism and the Protestant work ethic, western culture and its obsession with modern technology, Christianity and science, and the collective notion of reality.[3]

Says Stephanie Li, "For Morrison, storytelling and the process of writing are ways to explore the central challenges of human existence—how individuals both flourish and hurt one another, how oppression operates, how communities sustain generations.[4]

Focus on Community

Morrison writes about African Americans and their culture. She probes the heart of the dilemma facing many African Americans struggling to obtain prosperity and independence without severing the ancestral ties that nourish their African-American identities. But most importantly, she tells us a story of the human spirit: its strength, its endurance, and its ability to soar.[5]

Of her focus on community, Morrison explains:

In so many earlier books by African-American writers, particularly the men, I felt that they were not writing to me. But what interested me was the African-American experience throughout whichever time I spoke of. It was always about African-American culture and people— good, bad, indifferent, whatever—but that was, for me, the universe.[6]

Spotlighting Race

Race relations is a hot topic for Morrison. She focuses on how racism evolved and impacts African Americans. All of the major works discussed here—*The Bluest Eye*, *Song of Solomon*, and *Beloved*—revolve around racial issues.

These works also confirm one thing: Morrison's writing is edgy. She writes about topics that many authors avoid. She neither preaches nor pacifies. Readers choose whether to agree or disagree with viewpoints expressed by her main characters. Trudier Harris argues, "Nationally, we certainly owe Toni Morrison more than mere groupie applause. She has been in the forefront of stamping diversity upon the face of American literature."[7]

It is not an accident that Morrison is in the forefront. She is a pioneering author who cares about race relations. Morrison says that she feels "personally sorrowful about black-and-white relations a lot of the time because black people have always been used as a buffer in this country between powers to prevent class war, to prevent other kinds of real conflagrations [fires or troubles]."[8]

Even though she cares about them, Morrison finds it hard to write about some issues. She felt that way about the legacy of slavery, which she focuses on in *Beloved*. In an interview she explains her feelings: "I had this terrible reluctance about dwelling on that era," she said. "Then I realized I didn't know anything about it, really, and I was overwhelmed by how long it was. Suddenly the time—300 years—began to drown me."[9]

She did not let the feeling stop her from writing *Beloved*. Many critics contend it is her best work. It reveals the many awful ways slaves were treated. It also looks at how they coped when first freed. Thus, *Beloved* compels readers to remember the trauma and horror of slavery and its lasting legacy in the United States.

She recalls, "I thought this has got to be the least read of all the books I've written because it is about something that the characters don't want to remember, I don't want to remember, black people don't want to remember, white people don't want to remember. I mean it's national amnesia."[10] Every time *Beloved* is read, the veil of amnesia lifts. Her dedication to those who lived as slaves guarantees they will not be forgotten.

Identity Lost or Found

Although the United States' history of racism and slavery is central to Morrison's body of work, her novels transcend these issues to envelop truths about the human condition, the problems we all face.[11]

Personal identity tops the list. Morrison examines this theme by looking at it in two ways. She reveals how people discover who they are. She also shows how characters can lose their sense of who they are.

In Morrison's works, identity is linked to names. Names offer clues to a character's personality or values. Sometimes a name may not be an appropriate one, but it fits somehow.

In *Song of Solomon*, for example, Milkman learns that his ancestor's real name is not Dead. The name was given to Milkman's ancestor by a drunken soldier. It is a perfect description for a family that is cold and uncaring.

Nicknames come into play, too. These names are often appropriate in Morrison's novels, denoting truths about character, revealing secrets, determining how a person is viewed by a particular community.[12] That is true in *Song of Solomon*. We learn that Milkman received his nickname because he was breast-fed too long, an apt choice for a man who feeds

WHAT'S IN A NAME?

Characters' names complement a book's setting, plot, and theme. They add suspense, fun, intrigue, magic, or other elements to a book. Sometimes they are tied to literary devices, like ambiguity, irony, or symbolism for extra effect. In *Song of Solomon* character names reflect some of these devices:

Irony. The author clues readers in about aspects of the character's life that do not live up to the name in some way. Ruth is a name of a biblical character admired by her rich husband. Morrison's "Ruth" is despised by her poor husband.

Symbolism. At times, the author uses a name that perfectly symbolizes the character's life, lifestyle, family, personality, or other characteristic. Morrison's use of the name "Dead" as her characters' last name, for example, symbolizes the family's "dead" relationships.

off others through so much of the story. Morrison also delves into spiritual topics, which may pinpoint another meaning of Milkman's name. First Corinthians, the book for which Milkman's sister is named, deals with the need for spiritual growth, referencing milk as a drink for spiritual babies.

Stephanie Li notes:

> Many aspects of the Dead family reflect Morrison's own history. The practice of choosing a child's name at random from the Bible is how Ramah [Morrison's mother] received her name. Moreover, the lyrics that the children sing in the concluding chapters of the novel and which lead Milkman to discover the history of his great-grandfather Solomon are based on a song from Morrison's family that begins, "Green, the only son of Solomon."[13]

The author associates solid food with being mature and milk with childishness. An immature person in this context could rightly be called a milkman. Looked at that way, Milkman's name is appropriate. In many ways he is an emotional child.

In Morrison's work there is often a search for identity. Characters struggle with the question, Who am I? Sometimes a quest is successful. Milkman's search changes his life. Other times the search is futile. Pecola Breedlove in *The Bluest Eye* is an example of a character who actually loses her identity. Pecola hates herself. She hates her culture. Like Pecola, others of Morrison's characters never rediscover their identity.

Pecola proves that the way a person views herself matters. Self-perception can hinder or help a search for identity. Morrison shows this by contrasting eyesight and vision. The first is simply the ability to see, a physical function. It is external and really does not have a great impact on a person's

Morrison speaks about her latest book with the Mocha Moms, a support group for at-home parents of color. Morrison's readers often say that they relate to the characters and struggles presented in her novels.

mind. The second refers to how people view themselves, others, and the world. Because vision is internal reflection, it is subjective. Pecola Breedlove's main problem was internal. She did not have a satisfactory or proper vision of herself.

Vision affects relationships. People whose vision of themselves is not satisfactory usually have a hard time bonding with others. Paul D in *Beloved* is a good example. He sees himself as having a tin heart. That vision causes him to avoid romantic relationships. Once his vision changes, he actively seeks Sethe's love.

Vision and beauty are linked in *The Bluest Eye*. Pecola believes she is ugly but longs to be pretty:

> It had occurred to Pecola some time ago that if her eyes, those eyes that held the pictures, and knew the sights—if those eyes of hers were different, that is to say, beautiful, she herself would be different. Her teeth were good, and at least her nose was not big and flat like some of those who were thought so cute. If she looked different, beautiful, maybe Cholly would be different, and Mrs. Breedlove too. Maybe they'd say, "Why, look at pretty-eyed Pecola. We mustn't do bad things in front of those pretty eyes."[14]

Intricate Relationships

The relationships in Morrison's works are complex. There is no ideal relationship. Morrison examines why this is the case. She often looks at female friendships and romantic love. Friendships between women are the focal point of *Sula*. Morrison quips, "I wrote *Sula* based on this theoretically brand-new idea: Women should be friends with one another."[15]

Morrison turns up the heat on romantic relationships in some of her novels. In *Song of Solomon*, for example, both

Hagar and Ryna lose their minds over the men they love. Susan Byrd tells Milkman, "You don't hear about women like that anymore, but there used to be more—the kind of woman who couldn't live without a particular man. And when the man left, they lost their minds, or died or something."[16] Byrd's words foreshadow Hagar's death. She dies of a broken heart after Milkman ruthlessly rejects her.

Before she dies, Hagar's crazed desire to kill Milkman draws community attention:

> Women watched her out of their windows. Men looked up from their checker games and wondered if she'd make it this time. The lengths to which lost love drove men and woman never surprised them. They had seen women pull their dresses over their heads and howl like dogs for lost love. And men who sat in doorways with pennies in their mouths for lost love. "Thank God," they whispered to themselves, "thank God I ain't never had one of them graveyard loves."[17]

"Graveyard love" is a term for a really bad relationship. It means to love someone so much, you do not care about anything else. It is, therefore, obsessive. When a person's love is not returned, he or she can become bitter or brokenhearted. Ryna was Hagar's ancestor. They both died from broken hearts. Their deaths demonstrate how some relationship problems can occur in multiple generations of one family. Morrison also explores this idea in other works.

Spirituality Explored

Beloved ranks high among Morrison's novels with a spiritual or supernatural theme. Beloved is a key character. She seems to be the ghost of a murdered child. Most characters—and readers—believe this is the case, but we cannot be certain.

True to her use of ambiguity, Morrison never confirms this assumption.

Beloved first haunts 124 Bluestone and later appears at the house as a twenty-year-old woman. She moves into 124. Her malicious, vindictive presence is obvious in the opening paragraph of the novel.

> 124 was spiteful. Full of a baby's venom. The women in the house knew it and so did the children. For years each put up with the spite in his own way, but by 1873 Sethe and her daughter Denver were its only victims.[18]

Venom is usually associated with snakes. Morrison introduces Beloved as a poisonous influence with the use of the word. She is a deadly connection to the past, causing more harm than good. Beloved's disappearance frees Sethe, Paul D, Denver, and the community from the guilt of the past. Remaining free of Beloved's consuming supernatural influence takes a conscious effort.

> So they forgot her. Like an unpleasant dream during a troubling sleep. Occasionally, however, the rustle of a skirt hushes when they wake, and the knuckles brushing a cheek in sleep seem to belong to the sleeper. Sometimes the photograph of a close friend or relative—looked at too long—shifts, and something more familiar than the dear face itself moves there. They can touch it if they like, but don't, because they know things will never be the same if they do.[19]

Besides ghosts and spirits, Morrison's treatment of spirituality or supernatural themes includes Christian and other religious beliefs. This spirituality is not necessarily portrayed as beneficial or accepted. *Paradise* is a good example. The story revolves around the fictional town of Ruby, Oklahoma.

The focus is on a run-down convent that is home to a community of women. Conflicts arise due to religious bigotry. Other issues come into play.

The Bluest Eye also examines spiritual themes. Soaphead Church calls himself a reader, adviser, and interpreter of dreams. His name and title appear to indicate a clean, spiritual, and moral life. Readers learn that this is not so. Soaphead Church is a phony. He has no powers.

Moreover, Soaphead shuns women but likes touching young girls' breasts. While Soaphead's actions are inappropriate, he sees them as innocent and tender. Indeed, in the present-day world, Soaphead would be considered a pedophile—an adult who inappropriately engages in some form of sexual contact with a minor.

Complex Sexuality

Morrison portrays sexual relations in both a positive and negative light. She addresses incest, rape, adultery, and other sensitive sexual topics. She does so to reveal characters' flaws. In *Song of Solomon*, Milkman's selfishness is evident. He does not respect women. He carelessly dumps them. He is especially cruel to his cousin Hagar. They have a sexual relationship for more than twelve years. One day he dumps her.

In *The Bluest Eye* we learn why Miss Della Jones's husband left her for another woman. She was too clean for him—sexually and spiritually.

> Well somebody asked him why he left a nice good church woman like Della for that heifer. You know Della always did keep a clean house. And he said the honest-to-God real reason was he couldn't take no more of that violet water Della Jones used. Said he wanted a woman

to smell like a woman. Said Della was just too clean for him.[20]

Room for Interpretation

Morrison has often been seen as a pioneer among women writers. Emerging in an era when African-American writing was seen as a predominantly male endeavor and women writers were perceived as predominantly white, she redefined the role of "black woman writer."[21] Critic Barbara Christian notes:

> The development of Afro-American women's fiction is, in many instances, a mirror image of the intensity of the relationship between sexism and racism in this country. And while many of us may grasp this fact in terms of economics or social status, we often forget the toll it takes in terms of self-expression and therefore self-empowerment. To be able to use the range of one's voice, to attempt to express the totality of self, is a recurring struggle in the tradition of . . . writers from the nineteenth century to the present.[22]

Since sex and race have been so interrelated in the history of the United States, it is not surprising that when black women published novels, they necessarily reflected on that relationship, whether they intended to or not.[23] But, says Professor Barbara Rigney, "Clearly there are no 'whole truths' or 'whole' men and women in Morrison's novels, at least not in any traditional fictional sense. Just as she challenges the dominant cultural view of language and signification, so Morrison also subverts traditional Western notions of identity and wholeness."[24]

Morrison's works have been studied by numerous critics. Some include Barbara Christian, Houston A. Baker Jr., and

Henry Louis Gates Jr. She faced the unrelentingly negative attitudes of many critics toward her work because, and she herself maintains, critics lack understanding of the culture, the world, the given quality out of which she writes.[25] A survey of the books and articles written about Morrison's work clearly indicates that hers is perceived to be among the most elusive in terms of interpreting and categorizing. Many different systematic critical approaches have been tried: existential, feminist, romantic, archetypal, or Marxist, just to name a few.[26]

Many critics consider Morrison primarily a feminist writer. This is because her works often center around women's experiences and are told from their viewpoints. Her work, therefore, does not rely on male-dominated views and traditional viewpoints of women's roles. According to author Maria Lauret:

> It was not until the demise of Black militancy in the early 1970s, when African-American feminists began to articulate their critiques of white feminism as well as Black gender relations, that a self-identified Black feminist cultural practice began to emerge in the work of Maya Angelou, Toni Morrison, Toni Cade Bambara, Gloria Naylor, and Alice Walker . . . [T]his new fiction differed from 1960s counter-cultural writing not only in its positive representation of strong black women, but perhaps particularly in its return to the language and rural setting of the American South and West as a "feminine" space, in contrast to the urban ghettos and street culture where their male literary peers found their inspiration.[27]

Morrison says she is not a feminist. When asked whether *Paradise* was a feminist novel, she replied, "Not at all. I would never write any 'ist.' I don't write 'ist' novels."[28] Her reasoning? She notes:

> In order to be as free as I possibly can, in my own imagination, I can't take positions that are closed. Everything I've ever done, in the writing world, has been to expand articulation, rather than to close it, to open doors, sometimes, not even closing the book—leaving the endings open for reinterpretation, revisitation, a little ambiguity. I detest and loathe [those categories]. I think it's off-putting to some readers, who may feel that I'm involved in writing some kind of feminist tract. I don't subscribe to patriarchy, and I don't think it should be substituted with matriarchy. I think it's a question of equitable access, and opening doors to all sorts of things.[29]

CREATIVE GENIUS: MORRISON'S BACKGROUND

Novelists know that each reader comes to the printed page with different expectations about the story. The expectations can drive how readers interpret the characters, setting, themes, and other parts of the book. Many writers worry about such interpretation. In a recent interview in *Hemispheres* magazine, Morrison said she is not concerned about that:

> It's like music. I remember music or songs I loved as a teenager which are just so boring and I cannot believe I liked them. And the opposite is also true. Music I thought was terrible, as I have aged, I've grown to appreciate. It's not that the song has changed—I have. I have different sensibilities, different interests, and so on.[1]

An Ohio Birthplace

Morrison was born on February 18, 1931, in Lorain, Ohio. She was born into a family of four children. Her parents were George and Ramah Wofford. They gave their second child the name Chloe Anthony. The poor couple was originally from the South. Her father moved to the North as a teenager. Her mother's family migrated to the North when she was a child. The cross-country moves were a means of seeking a better life, with more job opportunities and less racial tension.

Lorain was a racially mixed town. African Americans, Europeans, and Mexicans lived near each other. Times were tough for Morrison's family. The United States was still in the grip of the Great Depression. During that era, unemployment was high. Many banks and other institutions closed down. Morrison's father worked as much as he could, but jobs were scarce.

Something else was happening in the country. It was the end of the Harlem Renaissance. The era had opened doors for the future works of writers like Morrison. Years later, she would examine that time period in her writing.

Storytelling History

Morrison came from a family that shared oral stories. That foundation helped her to become a writer. She has said she was born into a family of storytellers and considers her father's folktales, her mother's singing, and her grandmother's number games all as examples of the uniquely African-American language she absorbed as a child.[2]

Storytelling comes alive in Morrison's work. For example, Sethe tells stories to Beloved. The tales help Beloved learn more about Sethe.

> It amazed Sethe (as much as it pleased Beloved) because every mention of her past life hurt. Everything in it was painful or lost. She and Baby Suggs had agreed without saying so that it was unspeakable; to Denver's inquiries Sethe gave short replies or rambling incomplete reveries. Even with Paul D, who had shared some of it and to whom she could talk with at least a measure of calm, the hurt was always there—like a tender place in the corner of her mouth that the bit left.[3]

Early School Years

Morrison once hoped to be a dancer. Her dream did not come true. She let the dream die. Morrison did well in school; in fact, she recalls being the only first grader in her class who could read. This strong academic beginning set the stage for Morrison's future success.

She was an honors student at Lorain High School. She enjoyed reading books by Russian, French, and English novelists. Her early favorites included the Russian writers Tolstoy and Dostoyevsky, French author Gustave Flaubert, and English novelist Jane Austen.[4]

Life at College

Morrison went on to attend Howard University in Washington, DC. The predominantly African-American school is one of the original historic black colleges and universities established for African Americans. The schools were needed because African-American students were barred from many colleges.

College proved a life-changing experience for Morrison in many ways. It was at Howard that she first became known as Toni. She decided to use the nickname because classmates had difficulty pronouncing her first name. Toni was a nickname for her middle name, Anthony, and much easier to pronounce than Chloe. She would eventually publish her fiction under this pseudonym.

Morrison pursued her love for literature. She studied English and American classics. She was pleased with her classes but dissatisfied with campus living. Unlike her, most students were more interested in socializing than studying. This was unsettling. She expected students to be more like bookworms than party animals. But college life soon improved. She joined the Howard University Players, a theater group that renewed Morrison's passion for drama. The group performed in on-campus drama productions during the

Students on the campus of Howard University in the 1940s. Morrison began attending the historically black school in 1949.

school year. In the summer they toured throughout the South performing various plays.

In 1953 Morrison graduated with a bachelor of arts degree in English. She also completed a minor in the classics. But Morrison's school days were not over. She dreamed of becoming a college professor. To do so, she had to continue her studies. She attended Cornell University in New York. She graduated in 1955 with a master of arts degree in English.

Morrison's first teaching job was in Texas. She taught English at Texas Southern University in Houston. She left there in 1957 for a job teaching English at her alma mater, Howard University. While working at Howard, Morrison joined a writers' group. It was a turning point in her life. One of the projects she completed in 1962 was a story about a young girl who wanted blue eyes. She later developed that story into *The Bluest Eye.*

Family Life

The move from Texas to Washington, DC, changed Morrison's life in another way. She met and married a Jamaican architect named Harold Morrison. The couple had two sons. Harold Ford Morrison was born in 1961. Slade Kevin Morrison was born three years later. He shared his mother's passion for writing and coauthored many books with her.

Morrison continued with the writing group. By this time, writing was not just a joy for Morrison, it was a way to escape her problems in her personal life. Her marriage was not a happy one, and it soon ended. Morrison and her husband divorced in 1964, when she was pregnant with Slade. She left Howard University, moving back home to Lorain, Ohio. She did not stay long. After her son was born, she took her family to upstate New York. She moved there for a new job, her first editing position with Random House publishers.

Two years later the family was on the move again. This time they headed to New York City. Morrison had accepted a new position at her company's headquarters. The new job as senior editor allowed her to work with many African-American authors. It helped Morrison decide to write a novel. *The Bluest Eye* was published in 1970.

pseudonym

A fictitious name by which a writer chooses to be known; a pen name.

Initially, she did not want to use Toni as a pen name. She submitted the novel under her nickname because it was most familiar to the editor. She forgot to tell him that she wanted Chloe to appear on the manuscript. Once *The Bluest Eye* was published, the name Toni Morrison stuck.

Morrison's fame grew. During the 1970s she published two new books and edited others. *Sula* was published in 1973. *Song of Solomon* was published in 1977. It won the National Book Critics Circle Award for fiction.

The 1980s were a decade of change for Morrison. She published *Tar Baby* in 1981. Then in 1983, she took a leap of faith. After working for Random House for twenty years, she resigned from her editing job, leaving to write full-time. In the years following, she would publish *Beloved* (1987), *Jazz* (1992), *Paradise* (1998), and *Love* (2003).

Writer as Teacher

Morrison found a way to combine her writing and teaching. She taught college classes at the State University of New York at Albany, Yale, and Bard College. In 1989 Morrison accepted a post with Princeton University. She became the first African-

Morrison began achieving literary success in the 1970s with the publication of her novels *The Bluest Eye*, *Sula*, and *Song of Solomon*. This photo shows the author in 1977.

American woman to hold a named chair at an Ivy League school.

A named chair is a specific professorship at a university that is named for the person or organization that sponsors and funds it or someone of their choice. It is generally awarded to a prominent professor in the field. Morrison was awarded a professorship named for a past president of Princeton. She later retired in 2006.

Literary Honors

Trudier Harris writes:

> By 1990 when Italy awarded Morrison the Chianti Ruffino Antico Fattore literary award, its highest literary honor, there were few scholars, students, or general American readers who were unfamiliar with her work. It was the first time the Italian prize, the equivalent of the American Book Awards, was granted to a black person or to a woman.[5]

Morrison has received many others honors. Her literary awards include the National Book Critics Circle Award (1977 for *Song of Solomon*), the Matrix Award (book category), and the Pulitzer Prize (1988 for *Beloved*). Other major awards include the 1996 National Book Foundation Medal for Distinguished Contribution to American Letters, the Pearl Buck Award (1994), the title of Commander of the Order of Arts and Letters (Paris, 1994), and the 1978 Distinguished Writer Award from the American Academy of Arts and Letters.[6]

Morrison made history again in 1993. She was the first African-American woman to be awarded the Nobel Prize for Literature. Trudier Harris was correct in predicting that the honor would be partly responsible for making Morrison's works more and more popular:

FAMILY Affair

Authors don't always have children who like to write. Toni Morrison's son did, though, and wrote books with his famous mother. Their Who's Got Game? series is based on Aesop's Fables. These stories were written thousands of years ago and feature basic lessons and themes about life. The mother-son writing team also wrote several other books, including *Peeny Butter Fudge*. That book features siblings making fudge with their grandmother and includes a recipe at the end of the book. Slade Morrison died in 2010.

The Nobel Prize in Literature will mean that Morrison's works will be ever more popular and ever more available. It means that an African American writer who may once have been viewed as writing against the grain of American literature will be more centrally incorporated into it, indeed acclaimed in a variety of ways. It means that a woman, writing in English, has been recognized as equal to the best writers worldwide. It means that Morrison will become even more the representative artist/spokesperson for African American writers, as Richard Wright was in the 1940s, James Baldwin after him, Ralph Ellison briefly thereafter, and Alice Walker in the 1980s.[7]

Morrison was awarded the National Humanities Medal in 2000. The winners of this award are named by the president of the United States, who was Bill Clinton at the time. The announcement noted:

The 2000 National Humanities Medalists are distinguished individuals who have made extraordinary contributions to American cultural life and thought ... Through their powers of creativity and vision, the National Humanities Medalists are helping to preserve, interpret and expand the nation's cultural heritage. Their work represents an invaluable public service.[8]

In addition to the many awards bestowed upon Morrison over the years, she has also been the recipient of numerous honorary degrees from colleges and universities. These include Harvard, the University of Pennsylvania, Sarah Lawrence, Dartmouth, Yale, Georgetown, Columbia, and Brown.[9]

Time to Write

Morrison was pregnant when her marriage dissolved. As a single mom, she had a demanding schedule. However, Morrison found time to write. Ann Geracimos explains that "[Morrison] started writing fiction on the kitchen table at odd hours when her children were in bed."[10]

Of her schedule, Morrison says, "I do get up very early, embarrassingly early, before there is light, and I write . . . before that, I've spent a couple of years, probably eighteen months, just thinking about these people, the circumstances, the whole architecture of the book."[11]

Morrison used her time on the New York City subway to think about and plot her novels. As soon as she could, she would write down her thoughts. Morrison explains that she tries "to write when I'm not teaching, which means Fall and most of the Summer."[12]

Morrison wrote about issues and situations that she was passionate about. She has said that she wrote the type of books that she longed to read. She did not care if the themes were controversial. Initially *The Bluest Eye* was not well received, because of its focus on race relations between African Americans and Caucasians. But that did not stop Morrison from writing about the topic again.

She does not worry about writer's block, a psychological condition that interrupts a writer's ability to work. Morrison believes that when the condition strikes her, it is because she is uncertain about the direction of a work. Instead of forcing herself to write, she waits patiently until she has the solution to the particular problem.

Primary Influences

Morrison's family was a powerful influence on her career. Her mother's singing and her grandmother's storytelling were key. Harris notes:

> When all the reading is done, when all the stories are told, what remains is language, Morrison's superior ability to weave tales, her uncanny skill at giving distinctive voices to a variety of characters across class, race, and education levels. Scholars and readers have repeatedly commented on Morrison's storytelling ability, and credit the gift in part to the tradition of oral storytelling that surrounded her growing up in Ohio.[13]

thesis

A thorough written analysis of a specific subject that students in graduate school must complete.

Morrison was also influenced by the works of William Faulkner, which she studied in graduate school. She wrote her master's thesis on the works of Faulkner and Virginia Woolf, another acclaimed novelist. A thesis is like a term paper. It analyzes a specific subject. Graduate students must complete a thesis before receiving their degree. Faulkner wrote novels, short stories, and poems. He received the Nobel Prize for Literature in 1949.

Faulkner wrote about race relations, too. One of Faulkner's primary themes is the abuse of African Americans by Southern whites. Because Faulkner's novels deal with the decay and anguish of the South following the Civil War, they abound in violent and sordid events. But they are grounded in a profound and compassionate humanism that celebrates the tragedy, energy, and humor of ordinary human life.[14] Morrison

Morrison studied the works of William Faulkner, pictured here, which shared similar themes to those of Morrison.

follows in Faulkner's footsteps. She addresses similar issues, concerns, and themes.

Southern Flair

Morrison's novels are set in diverse places. There is, nonetheless, a strong Southern influence in her work. Four factors may apply: First, Morrison's family has Southern roots. Second, the South is prominent in Faulkner's works. Third, thousands of African Americans migrated from the North to the South:

> [I]n the movement north, blacks not only migrated to large cities, as so much of Afro-American literature indicates, but to small towns as well. The effect of such a migration on the characters of the novel is a major thematic consideration in *The Bluest Eye*.[15]

A fourth reason may be the major role that racial issues have played in the South:

> Slavery was known as the "peculiar institution" of the South and was protected by the Constitution of the United States ... When differences with the North, especially over the issue of the extension of slavery into the federal territories, ultimately appeared insoluble, the South turned (1860–61) the doctrine of states' rights into secession (or independence), which in turn led inevitably to the Civil War. Most of the major battles and campaigns of the war were fought in the South, and by the end of the war, with slavery abolished and most of the area in ruins, the Old South had died.[16]

Morrison revisits the Old South in *The Bluest Eye*. The book secured her literary career and endeared Morrison to readers. Trudier Harris contends:

> In the worlds she has traveled and in the worlds she has created, Toni Morrison has left her imprint upon our

imaginations. She has taught us the futility of thinking only in absolutes, for we cannot facilely [easily] conclude that Cholly Breedlove is a beast for raping his daughter, or that Sethe is morally guilty even as we know that she killed her child. She has taught us to trust ancestry and intuition, as Pilate Dead and Baby Suggs do, to wonder about the boundaries between this and other realms, and indeed to push these boundaries as far as we can. She has taught us to see and to question our preconceptions of negligence, racism, deception, evil, and the supernatural—all with the vividness of biblical images unfolding in the mind of a Baptist preacher.[17]

RECLAIMING RACIAL BEAUTY: *THE BLUEST EYE*

Toni Morrison did not dream of being a writer when she was a child. Rather, she wanted to be a reader! She explains:

> I thought everything that needed to be written had already been written or would be. I only wrote the first book because I thought it wasn't there, and I wanted to read it when I got through. I am a pretty good reader. I love it. It is what I do really. So, if I can read it, that is the highest compliment I can think of.[1]

Morrison's first book was *The Bluest Eye*. The main character is Pecola Breedlove. She is a poor, unattractive African-American girl. She thinks blue eyes will make her beautiful and popular. Pecola is eleven years old. For as long as she can remember, no one noticed her. So she prays for blue eyes. She wants the bluest blue eyes available to mankind, believing they would solve all of her problems. She would be loved, not ignored. She would see pretty things, act pretty, and live prettily ever after.

Better in Blue?

Why would an African-American girl want blue eyes? That is the crux of *The Bluest Eye*. The novel tackles a difficult subject: racial prejudice and its impact on the victim. It focuses on stereotypes, beauty in particular. Pecola Breedlove struggles to survive in a society that glorifies whiteness. She prays for

Morrison completed the story that would become *The Bluest Eye* in the early 1960s, when the country was in the midst of the civil rights movement. That struggle inspired her to explore the idea of racial beauty in her story.

blue eyes because she associates them with beauty, love, and acceptance.

Author Valerie Boyd notes that "Morrison's first novel takes place in 1941, when Pecola, an innocent and convenient victim of her community's frustration, anger, ignorance, and shame, becomes a woman. Raped by her father, she gives birth to a stillborn child and then escapes her sense of ugliness into madness, convinced that she has magically been given blue eyes."[2]

> **stereotype**
>
> A standard used to define a thing, idea, image, or opinion in an oversimplified or prejudicial manner.

Morrison shares her reasons for developing Pecola's character as she did.

> In trying to dramatize the devastation that even casual racial contempt can cause, I chose a unique situation, not a representative one. The extremity of Pecola's case stemmed largely from a crippled and crippling family—unlike the average black family and unlike the narrator's. But singular as Pecola's life was, I believed some aspects of woundability were lodged in all young girls. In exploring the social and domestic aggression that could cause a child to literally fall apart, I mounted a series of rejections, some routine, some exceptional, some monstrous, all the while trying to avoid complicity in the demonization process Pecola was subjected to. That is, I did not want to dehumanize the characters who trashed Pecola and contributed to her collapse.[3]

Morrison first captured the idea in a short story. Two factors led her to expand it into a novel. She was "inspired by the larger civil rights struggle and by the efforts of blacks to reclaim what she calls their 'racial beauty.'"[4] She also was inspired by something that wasn't happening much in 1965: the publication of novels by black women. Such books were few and far between—or out of print, as was the case with the works of Zora Neale Hurston, the most prominent black female writer of the first half of the twentieth century. In an interview in the 1983 collection *Black Women Writers at Work*, Morrison explained that she wrote *The Bluest Eye* and *Sula* . . . because "they were books I had wanted to read. No one had written them yet, so I wrote them."[5]

Morrison says that the idea for the book was sparked by a situation from her childhood. She vividly remembers being disgusted by a schoolmate's desire to have blue eyes. In the afterword to the Plume 1994 edition of *The Bluest Eye*, Morrison recalls:

> We had just started elementary school. She said she wanted blue eyes. I looked around to picture her with them and was violently repelled by what I imagined she would look like if she had her wish. The sorrow in her voice seemed to call for sympathy, and I faked it for her, but, astonished by the desecration she proposed, I "got mad" at her instead.[6]

The story is also about the Breedloves' adjustment to urban living. The family had lived in a rural, Southern community. Expectations were high that the move would be positive. It proved otherwise. Barbara Christian describes the Breedloves:

> Recent arrivals to this town whose connection to another place, the South, had been intense and life sustaining if only because they'd had to forge a tradition of survival against great odds. As new inhabitants, and as black people, they are looked down upon by the more established white community of Lorain, Ohio. The black migrants must therefore learn how to survive in

this land that is at present a sterile one for them, even as they try to evolve a tradition that is functional in this place. Until they do, their lives will lack coherence.[7]

Cholly Breedlove finds work in a steel mill, while Pauline, his wife, stays at home. Pauline cannot relate to other African-American women. Regional differences between the South and the North make it difficult for Pauline to do so. Christian explains:

> Separated from the rural South, which allowed her privacy and freedom of imagination, and cut off from the tradition of her maternal ancestors, she falls prey to the destructive ideas of physical beauty and romantic love as measures of self-worth. Her life in urban Lorain, Ohio removes her from her customary avenues for expressing herself and for wrestling some meaning out of life. As a result she lays the blame for her misfortunes on her incapacity as a black woman to be beautiful and therefore unworthy of a good life.[8]

Because she is lonely, Pauline depends more and more on Cholly, which he does not like. Pauline's desire to impress other women causes her to ask for money from her husband. When he cannot not provide it, she gets a job. Money issues turn their happy marriage violent. "Money became the focus of all their discussions, hers for clothes, his for drink. The sad thing was that Pauline did not really care for clothes and makeup. She merely wanted other women to cast favorable glances her way."[9]

Effect of White Ideals

Rejection from other women rocks Pauline's self-esteem. They do not like Pauline's hair because she does not straighten it.

They are also cruel to Pauline for other reasons. Their actions cause her to resent her African-American heritage.

Philosopher Cornell West contends that *"The Bluest Eye* . . . reveals the devastating effect of pervasive European ideals of beauty on the self-image of young African-American women. Morrison's exposure of the harmful extent to which these white ideals affect the black self-image is a first step toward rejecting these ideals and overcoming the nihilistic self-loathing they engender in blacks."[10]

Like her mother, Pauline, Pecola does not think well of herself. However, she adores Shirley Temple. Pecola adores the perky, blond-haired, blue-eyed child actress. She loves the Shirley Temple cup that she uses while staying with the MacTeers. It strengthens Pecola's desire for blue eyes.

Ignored by her teachers, despised by other adults, reviled by her classmates, and ultimately raped by her father, Pecola experiences ugliness in all its forms, retreating finally into her mad yearning to be the opposite of herself—that is, a white child like the universally *beloved* Shirley Temple, with the blondest hair and *the bluest eye*s.[11]

Themes

Valerie Boyd notes that in *The Bluest Eye*, "Toni Morrison tells an ugly story beautifully."[12] The three major themes of the novel are racial prejudice, racial superiority, and self-perception.

In the novel, most African Americans see white people as the more attractive race. They feel this way because of the media images they are exposed to. Newspapers, magazines, and movies mainly contain images of whites. They are good-looking, having fair skin tones, blond hair, and blue eyes. Few, if any, African Americans appear.

These images lead the African-American characters to believe that beauty depends on a person's skin color. It is a superficial definition of beauty. By these standards white (or light-skinned) is defined as "beautiful" and black (or dark-skinned), "ugly." The result is that most of the African-American characters hate themselves and other African-American people, especially dark-skinned individuals. Morrison calls this syndrome "racial self-loathing."[13]

Self-loathing comes up during interactions among African Americans. Light-skinned people are preferred. They are considered more attractive. They are also treated better. Whites reinforce this perception. They openly prefer lighter-toned African Americans. Consider Maureen Peal. Her white teacher treats her better than other students because she sees Maureen as prettier simply because of her fairer skin. Other children want to be her friend for the same reason.

Claudia MacTeer is immune to self-hate. This is shown in her attitude about Shirley Temple. Her sister, Frieda, and Pecola love the white actress. Claudia neither adores nor prefers her. One day Frieda serves Pecola graham crackers and milk in a black-and-white Shirley Temple cup. Claudia recalls,

> Frieda and she had a loving conversation about how cu-ute Shirley Temple was. I couldn't join them in their adoration because I hated Shirley. Not because she was cute, but because she danced with Bojangles, who was *my* friend, *my* uncle, *my* daddy, and who ought to have been soft-shoeing it and chuckling with me. Instead he was enjoying, sharing, giving a lovely dance thing with one of those little white girls whose socks never slid down under their heels.[14]

Racial superiority is the belief that one race is better than another. When people of one race are constantly told they are

In *The Bluest Eye*, popular child actress Shirley Temple is held up as the ideal of white beauty.

not as good as people of another race, they start believing it. They begin to hate their racial features and even their culture. Many times they feel ugly and worthless. Family and romantic relationships suffer.

Structure

Structurally, *The Bluest Eye* is divided into four sections—Autumn, Winter, Spring, and Summer. Each section begins with a paragraph from the Dick and Jane readers. The words become more and more disjointed with each section. Finally, words and sentences run together. There is no spacing or punctuation.

The Autumn section provides information about the Breedloves' apartment, home life, and personal and family struggles.

The second section is Winter. In this section Morrison gives us a glimpse of Geraldine and her son. She is a well-educated African-American woman. She turns her back on her race. Her son is an emotional mess. He tortures pets and bullies children. He is particularly abusive to Pecola.

In Morrison's Spring section she shares more information about Pauline and Cholly and the situations that shaped their lives, individually and as a couple. It is in this chapter that Pecola is raped. She also comes to believe that Soaphead Church has provided the magic for her to fulfill her dream of having blue eyes. This is not so. He has no powers. He is more devil than savior. Soaphead avoids women but enojys touching young girls. His actions are inappropriate and immoral, he views them as blameless and even kind. Soaphead could be considered a pedophile, in the setting of *The Bluest Eye*, such terminology had yet to be invented.

The Bluest Eye closes with Summer. While this season is usually one in which the earth is at its fullest and best, Pecola is at her worst. She, in her imagination, has received her blue eyes. Her imaginary friend confirms her delusion.

Narrative Style

The Bluest Eye is told from several points of views. One is that of an omniscient (all-knowing) narrator who shares information about characters and events. Claudia MacTeer provides two points of view: her first-person narrative from the perspective of a child is balanced by her retrospective outlook as an adult.

Plot Development

It is the summer of 1941 in Lorain, Ohio. The community is still suffering from the effects of the Great Depression. The MacTeers earn a few extra dollars by renting a room to a boarder. (A boarder is a person who pays to stay in someone else's home.) The MacTeers are poor, but they love one another. They are also willing to help others. They allow Pecola to stay with them for a short time. She arrives after her drunk father tries to burn down the building in which they live.

Pecola becomes friends with Claudia and Frieda MacTeer. Pecola is twelve, Claudia is nine, and Frieda is ten. Pecola enjoys getting to know the sisters. She has no other friends.

Each Breedlove is allegedly ugly. Claudia recalls, "No one could have convinced them that they were not relentlessly and aggressively ugly," adding, "You looked at them and wondered why they were so ugly; you looked closely and could not find the source. Then you realized it came from conviction, their conviction."[15, 16]

The Breedloves' poor self-image affects their relationships with each other and with the community. It spills over into how and where they live. Morrison explains,

> The Breedloves did not live in a storefront because they were having temporary difficulty adjusting to the cutbacks at the plant. They lived there because they were poor and black, and they stayed there because they believed they were ugly . . . It was as though some mysterious all-knowing master had given each a cloak of ugliness to wear, and they had each accepted it without question. The master had said, "You are ugly people." They had looked about themselves and saw nothing to contradict the statement; saw, in fact, support for it leaning at them from every billboard, every movie, every glance. "Yes," they had said. "You are right." And they took the ugliness in their hands, threw it as a mantle over them, and went about the world with it.[17]

Pecola and her family do not really fit into the community. They live in an old storefront that was once a furniture store. Pecola's father drinks too much and fights with his wife. Her parents' arguments make Pecola want to fade away. Her brother, Sammy, just runs away. Children and adults shun the Breedloves. Pecola becomes the one most dumped on.

Robert Sargent argues that "Pecola is both the communal and familial scapegoat—she is continually defined by other characters as 'Black and ugly.' She also embodies the insanity of trying to be white in order to be loved—in the end blue eyes are not sufficient; she must have *the bluest eyes*."[18]

People repeatedly call Pecola "black and ugly." The phrase comes across as a double insult and fuels her yearning for blue eyes. The final straw for the Breedloves begins when Pecola returns from her short stay with the MacTeers. She is developing into a young woman. She has experienced her first menstrual cycle. Her blossoming body is the only thing in Pecola's life that appears to be on track.

Plagued by the taunts of other children and unloved at home, Pecola seeks an escape. Pecola's humiliation peaks when her father rapes her. Her mother learns about the incestuous rape and beats Pecola.

Pecola becomes pregnant. Claudia and Frieda are not able to do anything about the most difficult situation Pecola faces, being pregnant with her father's child, but they wish that her unborn baby will survive. They go through a ritual of planting the seeds of marigolds as a magical act of solidarity with their pregnant friend.[19] Their faith is not sufficient. The seeds do not sprout. The baby dies.

Pecola desperately wants a miracle. She seeks the services of Soaphead Church. Like others, Pecola is unaware that he has no magical power. He is actually a religious con man. She asks him to change her eye color. Although he cannot, he devises a scheme to make her believe he can grant her wish. She believes his magic has worked and that she has blue eyes. Pecola, in essence, goes insane. Pecola also creates an imaginary friend. Only this friend can see Pecola's blue eyes.

Trudier Harris asserts:

> [Pecola's] journey from self-rejection to ultimate insanity in *The Bluest Eye* charts the course of the individual who finds herself outside of community norms, basically outside community caring. Although the adolescent Claudia, who alternately narrates the tale, and her sister, Frieda, do care about Pecola, their efforts, exemplified in the "magic" of sacrificing money earned from selling seeds in a childish attempt to alter Pecola's fate, are insufficient to save her.[20]

Character Development

The story is primarily centered around the Breedloves and the MacTeers. Soaphead Church is an essential secondary character.

Pecola Breedlove

Eleven-year-old Pecola, a symbol of the innocent victims of racial prejudice, yearns to be beautiful and accepted. "Long hours she sat looking in the mirror, trying to discover the secret of the ugliness, the ugliness that made her ignored or despised at school, by teachers and classmates alike."[21]

For Pecola, blue eyes are the epitome of beauty. She not only wants blue eyes—she wants the bluest. Pecola believes new eyes would become windows to an ideal world in which she would encounter only pleasant circumstances, experience acceptance rather than rejection, and be considered attractive rather than ugly. Unfortunately, such an ideal life remains outside of Pecola's reach.

> **epitome**
>
> The best example of a characteristic of something.

Pecola tries to escape the pain of watching her parents fight. She tries unsuccessfully to cope in different ways. Morrison writes, "Though the methods varied, the pain was as consistent as it was deep. She struggled between an overwhelming desire that one would kill the other, and a profound wish that she herself would die."[22] During one such fight Pecola begins to pray.

> "Please God," she whispered into the palm of her hand. "Please make me disappear." She squeezed her eyes shut. Little parts of her body faded away. Now slowly, now with a rush. Slowly again. Her fingers went, one by one; then her arms disappeared all the way to the elbow.

Her feet now. Yes, that was good. The legs all at once. It was hardest above the thighs. She had to be real still and pull. Her stomach would not go. But finally, it too went away. Then her chest and neck. The face was hard, too. Almost done, almost. Only her tight, tight eyes were left. They were always left.[23]

Cholly Breedlove

A violent alcoholic, Cholly is a bitter man. Ironically, he believes he is emotionally free. That is not the case. Cholly never overcomes being humiliated by two white men who caught him in his first sexual encounter. Cholly's displaced anger at the African-American girl—rather than the white men—carries over into his adult life and relationships.

At times, Cholly can be very tender, as he is when he first meets his wife, Pauline. He makes her feel beautiful by touching the foot other people try to avoid. Other times, he is very violent, especially when he is drunk. He rapes Pecola when he sees her washing dishes. The only thing on his mind is how Pecola reminds him of Pauline as a young woman.

Pauline Breedlove

Pauline Breedlove believes she is ugly. This is partly because she has a deformed foot. Feelings of isolation surfaced when Pauline moved from the South to Ohio, encountering rejection from other African Americans:

Northern colored folk was different too. Dicty-like. No better than whites for meanness. They could make you feel just as no-count, 'cept I didn't expect it from them. That was the loneliest time of my life. I 'member looking out at them from windows just waiting for Cholly to come home at three o'clock. I didn't even have a cat to talk to.[24]

Her self-hate makes it impossible for Pauline to really love her husband or children—and vice versa. Her family refers to her as Mrs. Breedlove. The formality reveals their chilly relationships. Pauline's employer calls her Polly. Barbara Rigney informs us that "the diminutive name is totally appropriate in this case, for Pauline has diminished herself through her obsequious dedication to whiteness just as surely as little Pecola is diminished by her desire for blue eyes."[25]

Despite her coldness, Pauline loves romantic movies, which are her form of escape. In the films she discovers another world, rich with emotional and physical contentment. The movies spark a love for white people in Pauline. That love enables her to love and highly esteem her white employers. At the same time, she despises and neglects her family. She takes great care of her employers' home but hardly cares for her own. Tender with her employers' daughter, Pauline treats Pecola harshly.

Claudia MacTeer

Claudia MacTeer is one of two sisters who befriends Pecola. She is a feisty, independent nine-year-old. Claudia willingly rejects the idea that beauty can only be defined by white standards. Thus, she is free from the self-loathing that other children and adults struggle with.

Frieda MacTeer

Frieda MacTeer is a year older than her sister, Claudia. She is more courageous. Yet she accepts society's definition of white-only beauty. Frieda is the one who decides to buy marigolds.

Soaphead Church

Soaphead Church is a fair-skinned man, originally from the West Indies. He describes himself as a "reader, adviser, and interpreter of dreams." Desperate people pay him to tell their fortunes and provide miracles. They never guess he is a con artist who has no real spiritual gifts. While women are interested in him, Soaphead is turned off by the touch of other people. He secretly likes young girls. But he never admits that touching them is a form of physical abuse.

Pecola asks Soaphead for the miracle of blue eyes. When she leaves, he pens a letter to God. He writes,

> I did what You did not, could not, would not do: I looked at that ugly little black girl, and I loved her. I played You. And it was a good show!
>
> I, I caused a miracle. I gave her the eyes. I gave her the blue, blue, two blue eyes. Cobalt blue. A streak of it right out of your own blue heaven. No one else will see her blue eyes. But *she* will. And she will live happily ever after. I, I have found it meet and right to do so.[26]

Soaphead's words are arrogant and illogical. He does not stop to think that his claim to have given Pecola blue eyes is impossible. Paul Weinstein contends, "In his letter to God, Soaphead Church challenges the religious definition of good and the origin of evil. Soaphead accuses God, the very embodiment (or disembodiment) of goodness. Not only does Soaphead refuse responsibility for his own actions, he succeeds in convincing himself that he is equal and finally superior to God."[27]

In addition to these characters, there are several minor ones who are noteworthy. They include China, Poland, and Marie, a trio of prostitutes who live above the Breedlove family. They accept Pecola as she is and are always willing to talk to her. Their tales of love and men intrigue Pecola. These shared tidbits are somewhat exaggerated for her. They contrast dramatically with Pecola's first encounter with sex. To Pecola the three prostitutes are friendly faces among the many hostile ones she sees. She does not clearly understand how other residents view the women. She has no clue that their relationships are not based on love. Thus, she never makes the connection that the women are vilified outsiders. They are not respected. In many ways they are not welcome.

Use of Literary Devices

Irony and symbolism are the two key literary devices used in *The Bluest Eye*.

Irony

Morrison's use of irony is reflected in her naming of some characters in *The Bluest Eye*, including the Breedloves. In their shabby home there is no breeding of love. There is no closeness. Instead, the environment, personal struggles, and other conditions actually breed the opposite. They breed contempt and self-loathing. They breed violence and bitterness. The family's surname may also serve as an allusion to Pecola's rape. Her father feels tenderness toward her before he attacks her.

Morrison also employs irony by naming each chapter after a season. The lives of the characters and the circumstances in the novel, however, often defy normal seasonal conditions. Pecola's life crumbles during summer, a time in which nature is normally at its fullest.

Symbols

Five significant symbols are the Dick and Jane series of books, homes/houses, blue eyes, marigolds, and outdoors.

The Dick and Jane series was used years ago to teach children to read. In the series the siblings were members of a happy, loving family. They lived with both parents and an adorable dog in a beautiful house. Morrison opens the book and each chapter with a paragraph from the series.

By beginning the novel this way, Morrison is setting up the house as a symbol. A symbol is something in a story that stands for or suggests another thing. In *The Bluest Eye* the type and condition of a family's home is a symbol of its social or financial status.

The Breedlove home may also reflect the family's character or emotional health. Dick and Jane live in a beautiful house with a happy, supportive family. The Breedloves, however, live in a decaying apartment. It is a symbol of their poverty. It may also hint at the declining nature of the family's interpersonal relations. According to Barbara Christian,

> From the ugly storefront of the Breedloves to the stan-dardized house of the Dick and Jane primer, the houses in this novel reflect the worth of the their inhabitants according to the norms of the society and emphasize the destructiveness of the hierarchical order . . . [T]he Breedloves fight and destroy each other in their ugly storefront because they come to believe in their own ugliness, their intrinsic unworthiness.[28]

The Dick-and-Jane series also symbolizes the negative change in characters' lives. Morrison distorts the paragraphs as the novel progresses. By the end of book, the words run together. It becomes impossible to decipher where sentences begin and end. Like the words, Pecola's life becomes squeezed. She is forced into maturity. She is boxed into impossible situations. Her life hardly resembles that of the young girl introduced in chapter one.

Another symbol used throughout the book is whiteness, which is associated with the Western world's standard of perfect beauty.

Blue eyes are an important symbol, representing self-hate and racial contempt. Pecola's desire for blue eyes reflects her poor self-image based solely on physical appearance. Pecola associates blue eyes with the beauty, social acceptance, and love enjoyed by middle-class white families.

Marigolds also play an important role in *The Bluest Eye*. Generally, seeds can represent hope as well as the continuing cycle of life. For Frieda and Claudia MacTeer the marigolds represent their hopes for Pecola's unborn baby. If the marigolds prosper, so will the baby. As children, they blame themselves when the marigolds fail to sprout. They mistakenly believe that their unfruitful efforts contributed to the baby's dying. As adults, they come to understand that this is not true. In retrospect, Claudia notes,

> Quiet as it's kept, there were no marigolds in the fall of 1941. We thought, at the time, that it was because Pecola was having her father's baby that the marigolds did not grow. A little examination and much less melancholy would have proved to us that our seeds were not the only ones that did not sprout; nobody's did. Not even the gardens fronting the lake showed marigolds that year. But so deeply concerned were we with the health and safe delivery of Pecola's baby we could only think of nothing but our own magic: if we planted the seeds, and said the right words over them, they would blossom, and everything would be all right.[29]

Morrison uses the term *outdoors* to symbolize homelessness and community separation. Claudia explains:

> Outdoors, we knew, was the real terror of life. The threat of being outdoors surfaced frequently in those days. Every possibility of excess was curtailed with it . . . To be put outdoors by a landlord was one thing—unfortunate,

Marigolds represent the life of Pecola's unborn child in *The Bluest Eye*.

In Her Own Words

You can hear Toni Morrison discuss her books, writing life, or other matters by connecting with the author herself. First, listen to lectures. Check to see if there are free lectures at local universities or other venues being broadcast online. Second, attend a book signing where you can hear the author read her work, buy the latest release, or perhaps take a photo with her. Third, view videos, like the ones from The Visionary Project (www.visionaryproject.org/morrisontoni/). In her interview for "The Colbert Report," Morrison says, "I know how to write forever. I don't think I could've happily stayed here in the world if I did not have a way of thinking about it, which is what writing is for me."[36]

but an aspect of life over which you had no control, since you could not control your income. But to be slack enough to put oneself outdoors, or heartless enough to put one's own outdoors—that was criminal.

There is a difference between being put *out* and being put *outdoors*. If you are put out, you go somewhere else; if you are put outdoors, there is no place to go. The distinction was subtle but final. Outdoors was the end of something, an irrevocable, physical fact, defining and complementing our metaphysical condition.[30]

Reviews

Reviews for *The Bluest Eye* appeared in such publications as *Newsweek* and the *Chicago Tribune*. They were mixed. In his favorable review in the *New York Times*, John Leonard wrote, "Miss Morrison exposes the negative of the Dick-and-Jane-and-Mother-and-Father-and-Dog-and-Cat photograph that appears in our reading primers, and she does it with a prose so precise, so faithful to speech and so charged with pain and wonder that the novel becomes poetry . . ."[31]

In the afterword to the Plume edition, however, Morrison notes, "With very few exceptions, the initial publication of *The Bluest Eye* was like Pecola's life: dismissed, trivialized, misread. And it has taken twenty-five years to gain her the respectful publication this edition is."[32]

The "respectful publication" Morrison refers to is the Plume edition of the novel, which was an Oprah's Book Club selection. It bore the club's logo, and Morrison appeared on Oprah Winfrey's national television show to discuss the novel.

After the book was showcased on the program, sales spiked. This was not the case with its original release. Actually, initial sales of *The Bluest Eye* were modest. Though not a major commercial success at the time, it is now seen as a landmark in American literature, signaling a shift from the white-dominated literary establishment and thus establishing the author's talent and her authoritative voice on the Afro-American experience: historically, sociologically, culturally, and otherwise.[33, 34]

Today, students continue to read *The Bluest Eye*. However, it continues to receive opposition:

> It was listed by the American Library Association as the fifteenth most commonly banned or challenged book during the years 2000–2009 for its sexual content and, at times, graphic subject matter. However, the book has long been considered to be an important contribution to American fiction for its powerful themes and literary merit.[35]

FREEDOM FLIGHT: SONG OF SOLOMON

S*ong of Solomon*, Morrison's third book, is a story about a man's search for personal identity. Its central theme is love. Writing the novel helped the author realize that she had the gift to be a writer. She explains in her *Paris Review* interview: "It was by the time I was writing *Song of Solomon* . . . that I began to think that this was the central part of my life."[1] For her, it was an important discovery because many women writers had difficulty succeeding in the literary field. She explained, "Well, it isn't difficult anymore, but it certainly was for me and for women of my generation or my class or my race."[2]

Critics and readers adored *Song of Solomon*. Published in 1977, it won the National Book Critics Circle Award. Morrison became viewed as an author worth celebrating.

Narrative Style

Morrison tells the story from a man's perspective. As a woman writer, Morrison found it difficult to write this way. She succeeded by using the men in her family as models. Morrison drew from her personal history; the story of Solomon Willis, her grandfather, is the source of this work.[3]

Themes

The most important themes of *Song of Solomon* are love and the search for personal identity. The two themes are closely tied. Milkman, one of the chief characters, discovers the

Morrison is seen here in 2012 posing with her 1977 novel, *Song of Solomon.*

connection between love and personal identity. Milkman must learn to love himself and others. Only then will he discover who he is and why his life matters.

Structure

The novel is divided into two parts. The first part details Milkman's life before his life-altering trip. The second focuses on his trip, which leads to Milkman's discovery of his family's roots and newfound self-esteem.

The book begins and ends with men leaping off high places: Mr. Smith in part one; Milkman in part two. Morrison brings the book full circle with the related incidents. Readers realize, however, that the two men are very different.

Language

Song of Solomon is a mix of many types of language. References are made to Greek mythology, African folklore, and biblical texts.

In *Song of Solomon* the use of language matches each character's background. Guitar's rough language denotes his preference for hanging out in the street. It exemplifies the tough persona he adopted over time.

> While Milkman is associated with flying, Guitar . . . is identified with the earth. A natural hunter, he misses the smells and sounds of the woods he had known in the South. He has the clarity of the earth. But like the earth, which is turned soggy with the blood of racism, he is maimed. He uses his natural capacity as a hunter to try to change the situation in which he and his people are caught, and his involvement with The Seven Days is his way of balancing the generations of blacks killed by whites. But in doing so, he must also snuff out his other

natural instincts until he becomes totally absorbed with earthy solutions to the evils that surround him.[4]

Plot Development

Song of Solomon begins with the death of Robert Smith. The African-American insurance agent commits suicide by jumping off the roof of the town's whites-only hospital. Wearing blue silk wings, he claims he can fly. His artificial wings carry him downward to a painful death.

His death is ironic, as his job was selling life insurance. Money from insurance policies helps people pay for funeral costs and other expenses incurred when a loved one dies. The insurance provides a sense of security. It is far more durable and stable than Mr. Smith's fake wings.

The day after Mr. Smith's leap, Ruth Dead goes into labor. She is admitted at Mercy Hospital, becoming the first African-American person ever treated there. Her newborn son, named Macon after his father, is the first African American born at the hospital. The boy is later nicknamed Milkman.

Like Mr. Smith, Milkman is fascinated with flying.

> Mr. Smith's blue silk wings must have left their mark, because when the little boy discovered, at four, the same thing Mr. Smith had learned earlier—that only birds and airplanes could fly—he lost all interest in himself. To have to live without that single gift saddened him and left his imagination so bereft that he appeared dull even to the women who did not hate his mother.[5]

Milkman's disinterest leads to selfishness. He takes advantage of his family and has few friends. His attitude changes somewhat when he meets Guitar Bains. Guitar is a few years older than Milkman. Poor and streetwise, Guitar introduces

Milkman to a life different from the privileged one he has been living.

Through Guitar, Milkman finally meets his aunt, Pilate, and cousins, Reba and Hagar. Milkman is hooked. He begins visiting Pilate's household quite often. Eventually, Milkman has sexual relations with Hagar. The relationship lasts for more than twelve years.

With few other prospects, Milkman reluctantly joins his father's business. His job is to collect rent from tenants. It fits him perfectly, enabling Milkman to do whatever he wants. At age thirty-two Milkman becomes dissatisfied with his life and desires a change. Moving out of his parent's home becomes his primary goal.

Unfortunately, Milkman has no personal wealth. He gets his money from his father, who later provides a solution to Milkman's dilemma. Macon tells Milkman that he believes Pilate is hiding gold in her house. If Milkman agrees to steal the gold, he can have one-half of all money received when the gold is exchanged for cash. Milkman agrees to the plan, inviting Guitar to help him. He promises Guitar one-third of the profits.

The adventure begins. The friends succeed in grabbing the bag, but to their surprise they actually find a skeleton. Ultimately, the search for gold spurs Milkman's complete transformation. The gold serves as both a blessing and a curse.

The blessing is that Milkman gets a new outlook on life. He finally learns to bond with other African-American men and even has a tender relationship with a woman. He also revisits his ancestral home so Pilate can bury her father's bones. All of these events are indicative of Milkman's newfound maturity.

The gold becomes a curse as it destroys Milkman's only friendship. Greed makes Guitar want to kill Milkman.

He falsely believes his friend will cheat him. His first few attempts to kill Milkman fail. He later tries again but ends up murdering Pilate. As she dies, Milkman finally realizes that his aunt always had the capacity to fly. In other words, she was always emotionally free. Her love sustained her flight. Angry at Guitar and ready to spread his wings, Milkman leaps for Guitar. The novel ends.

At the end of the novel, Milkman is more hero than villain, more caring than selfish. It is unlikely that with a newfound sense of identity and purpose, Milkman would commit suicide. Yet readers cannot be certain. Morrison purposely concludes *Song of Solomon* on an ambiguous note. It is unclear whether or not Milkman leaps to his death. It is left to the reader to decide whether he dies, fights or murders Guitar, or soars away like his great-grandfather Solomon. What is clear is that Milkman has experienced the joy of flying and the related freedom he has long desired. He is free for the first time in his life.

Character Development

Milkman Dead

Milkman is the protagonist. At the novel's beginning, Milkman leads a self-centered, noncommitted life. As the only son of a wealthy landowner, Milkman is born into what should have been the ideal American family. His mother stays at home. His father owns a prosperous real estate business. They own a home. But money cannot buy love. Family members are cold and noncommunicative. Milkman's father is also stingy and mean. He abuses his wife for years, until Milkman retaliates. Because of his family background, Milkman feels alienated and unloved.

These feelings spill over into his relationships. He has a tough time making friends and takes advantage of women. Guitar Bains, who is the antithesis of Milkman, becomes Milkman's best friend. But a search for gold later destroys their friendship.

From an early age Milkman is selfish and conceited:

> He avoided commitment and strong feelings, and shied away from decisions. He wanted to know as little as possible, to feel only enough to get through the day amiably and to be interesting enough to warrant the curiosity of other people—but not their all-consuming devotion.[6]

Milkman's life-changing quest for gold leads him to his ancestral hometown. One important change is Milkman's new ability to connect

antithesis
The exact opposite.

with others. Now a man in the fullest sense of the word, Milkman willingly takes responsibility for his actions.

Guitar Bains

Milkman's only friend, Guitar Bains, is a street-smart teen when he first meets Milkman. The name Guitar stuck with him because he longed for one when he was a child but never got it. The name is appropriate because he goes through life longing for the unattainable. Unlike Milkman, Guitar grew up poor. He introduces Milkman to some of his bad habits, including drinking.

Guitar grows from a cocky teenager into a very angry man. He is upset about racist crimes against his people. He eventually joins the Seven Days, a militant group of seven African-American men who avenge the deaths of other African Americans. They do so by killing innocent whites.

A crowd exits the funeral for an African-American girl killed in the bombing of a Birmingham, Alabama, church in 1963. In *Song of Solomon*, Guitar and the Seven Days murder innocent white people in retaliation for racist violence like the Birmingham bombing.

They are copycats. They try to reenact murders that whites committed.

Guitar's preoccupations with avenging murders and with gold alter his life. He loses focus, becoming more committed to the Seven Days and the group's retaliation efforts. Robert Smith's suicide in the beginning of the novel and Guitar's crazed search for gold prove that the Seven Days' tactics may not be as successful as members believe. Trudier Harris notes:

> From using the murder of Emmett Till in Mississippi in 1955 as a backdrop, to the bombing of a church in Birmingham, Alabama, in 1963 that left four little black girls dead, Morrison explores racism and race relations, asserting that the retaliatory violence of the kind that the black vigilante group, the Seven Days, wants to perpetuate against whites is finally unacceptable.[7]

Macon Dead Jr.

Macon has lots of money, but no friends. Mean and arrogant, Macon is hated by family members, tenants, and others in the community. His wife and children secretly despise him—for good reason:

> Solid, rumbling, likely to erupt without prior notice, Macon kept each member of his family awkward with fear. His hatred for his wife glittered and sparked in every word he spoke to her. The disappointment he felt in his daughters sifted down on them like ash, dulling their buttery complexions and choking the lilt out of what should have been girlish voices. Under the frozen heat of his glance they tripped over doorsills and dropped the salt cellar into the yolks of their poached eggs. The way he mangled their grace, wit, and self-esteem was the single excitement of their days. Without

the tension and drama he ignited, they might not have known what to do with themselves.[8]

Macon is a true American capitalist, as he loves owning property. That fondness dates back to his childhood. Macon witnessed his father's murder by white men intent on stealing the family's land. Afterward, he defines wealth as having land and buildings. He uses his wealth to impress others. It does not work. Townspeople, for example, speak of his expensive car as a hearse, a reference to his last name and personality.

Macon and his sister, Pilate, have not spoken for years due to a mystery surrounding gold they discovered as children. Ironically, the "gold" is really their father's bones, which Pilate keeps in a tarp hanging over her bed. To Pilate, who treasures relationships, the bones are priceless; to Milkman they are worthless.

Ruth Dead

Ruth Dead is the only child of the town's first African-American doctor. Her family gave her the very best education in hopes that she would marry well. Ruth's father agrees to her marriage with Macon. The marriage is a disaster.

Over the years Ruth feels continually lonely and rejected. She comes to the conclusion that her father is the only person who has ever really loved her. Her marriage breaks down due, in part, to an event related to her father's death. Her husband's anger leads to abuse. Morrison writes that Ruth "began her days stunned into stillness by her husband's contempt and ended them wholly animated by it."[9] Ruth's feelings of rejection and loneliness cause her to breast-feed Milkman far longer than necessary. She also copes by frequently visiting her father's grave.

Magdalene (Lena) and Corinthians Dead

Milkman's sisters, Lena and Corinthians, as they are called, are unmarried. They make red velvet roses by hand, which keeps them occupied when they are children. Their parents expect them to marry one day, but that does not happen. While Corinthians is considered a good catch, she appears too passive and elegant for most men.

> She was pretty enough, pleasant enough, and her father had the money they could rely on if needed, but she lacked drive. These men wanted wives who could manage, who were not so well accustomed to middle-class life that they had no ambition, no hunger, no hustle in them. They wanted their wives to like the climbing, the acquiring, and the work it took to maintain status once it was achieved. They wanted wives who would sacrifice themselves and appreciate the hard work and sacrifice of their husbands.[10]

Like Denver in *Beloved*, Corinthians only discovers satisfaction when she moves beyond the comfort of home. For Corinthians, that encompasses employment and a love relationship. The idea of self-sufficiency, especially for women, is a theme found in other Morrison works.

Pilate

Pilate is Macon's unusual sister. The two have not spoken in years for two reasons. First, Macon believes she stole gold. Second, Macon dislikes Pilate's lifestyle, mannerisms, and sloppy appearance.

Pilate and her brother are very different. Macon's life is ruled by money and property. Pilate's life focuses on intangible values—love, respect, family, and loyalty. Macon regards family ties as unimportant; Pilate fiercely protects her daughter and granddaughter, who live with her.

In *Song of Solomon*, Pilate represents the stereotypical strong African-American woman. She is independent and daring. Pilate does not live up to society's expectations. Her main source of income comes from illegally brewing and selling alcohol from her run-down shack. To many people, Pilate is simply eccentric, but to Milkman she is a source of inspiration. Pilate is killed by Guitar while on a trip with Milkman to bury her father's bones.

Hagar

Hagar, Pilate's granddaughter and Milkman's cousin, has a long-term relationship with Milkman. The fact that they are cousins fails to prevent them from becoming involved. Hagar loves Milkman so much that their relationship becomes a measure of her self-worth. She is angry when Milkman breaks up with her after more than twelve years. To get his attention and stay in contact with him, she unsuccessfully tries to murder him. Finally, she dies of a broken heart.

Reba

Reba is Pilate's only child and Hagar's mother. She is known to be very lucky at contests but unlucky in love. The greatest prize she ever wins is a diamond ring in a Sears, Roebuck contest. She actually wins first prize, but because she is African American, the store chooses a second "first place" winner. Reba wears the diamond around her neck until she sells it to pay for Hagar's final shopping spree.

Literary Devices

Morrison employs irony and symbolism in *Song of Solomon*. One example of how Morrison uses irony is in the naming of

Mercy Hospital. The town's whites-only medical facility, the hospital refuses to provide health care services to African Americans—hence its nickname, Not Mercy Hospital.

Important symbols woven into the novel include red velvet roses, flying, Pilate's navel, money, and names.

Ruth and her daughters make red velvet roses, selling them to various stores. The roses symbolize artificial relationships that may occur in romantic love, family life, and friendships.

Flying is a symbol of freedom, abandonment, and wholeness. Through flying, characters can achieve freedom from something in their past, present, or future. Conversely, characters can also abandon whatever is holding them back and causing them not to fly. In order for Milkman's ancestor Shalimar to fly, he abandons his wife and children. In similar fashion Milkman abandons Hagar as he flies off to search for his ancestral roots. In both cases the women left behind are devastated. Each dies of a broken heart.

Finally, characters can experience emotional wholeness or completeness through flying. *Song of Solomon* begins and ends with an African-American man trying to experience freedom from societal restrictions by actually flying. In the beginning, Robert Smith leaps to his death from the roof of Mercy Hospital. At the end of the novel, Milkman jumps off Solomon's Leap, heading toward Guitar, who has just killed Pilate. According to legend, Milkman's great-grandfather had jumped from the same location, flying back to Africa.

The legend surrounding Milkman's great-grandfather makes it easy to believe that Pilate has no navel. When Pilate's mother dies during childbirth, the umbilical cord fully detaches without needing to be cut. Upon discovering her secret, many people fear her. Others shun her. Pilate adapts by keeping her stomach hidden. She even hides it from the men she has relationships with.

In the novel a navel represents human life and dependence on others. Pilate's lack of a navel symbolizes her independence from others. She is self-sufficient, as evidenced by her isolated home and her liquor-brewing business. Barbara Christian writes, "Pilate is presented in the novel as the healer of the spirit, the guide to essences beyond outward appearance or material things. But without a navel, she learns how important, though misleading, appearances are to people. Thus, she learns to rely on inner qualities rather than outer manifestations."[11]

The absence of a navel not only gives Pilate an aura of magic and mystery but also gives Morrison a way of accounting for Pilate's experimental approach to life. From a naturalistic perspective, the fact that Pilate has no navel shocks others and has the effect of isolating her from ordinary folk. Therefore, she is forced to see the world from her own point of view. From a symbolic perspective the lack of a navel suggests "that she had not come into this world through normal channels, that she has given birth to herself, in the sense that she has shaped herself as a unique individual."[12]

Money as a symbol of a person's good or bad character magnifies what already exists in that person's heart. Macon is as mean, selfish, and cruel as he is rich. He has plenty of money but still wants to rob his sister to get gold. For Macon, money represents unquenchable desire. Interestingly, "Song of Solomon" in the Bible was written by one of the wealthiest kings who ever lived. He was also one of the wisest. King Solomon, however, discovered that chasing money and women does not bring happiness.

The Bible's "Song of Solomon" is traditionally credited to King Solomon, ancient king of Israel. Many other biblical references appear in the novel, particularly in the naming of characters like Pilate, Corinthians, and Magdalene.

Meanwhile, the names or nicknames of characters or places also have special meaning in *Song of Solomon*. Trudier Harris notes:

> From a drunken Yankee mistakenly writing down the family surname as "Dead," to "Not Doctor Street," the avenue on which Milkman is born, to Pilate Dead, the aunt who guides Milkman to maturity, to an assortment of other names, nicknames, and pieces of names, Morrison [emphasizes the need] for understanding personal and communal history.[13]

Milkman's first and last name, Pilate, and Mercy Hospital are some of the names that hold great significance in the novel. We discover that Dead is an appropriate name for a family that has difficulty loving themselves and others. "In short," writes Patrick Bryce Bjork, "the atmosphere surrounding the Dead family hardly constitutes what one might call a loving and warm one but is, instead, cold and cruelly comical."[14]

Milkman's grandfather could not read. He chose names for his children by pointing to ones in the Bible. When he chooses Pilate, the midwife tries to change his mind. She explains that in the Bible, Pilate was one of the persons responsible for the crucifixion of Jesus Christ. Macon Dead thinks it is the perfect name. His wife dies giving birth to Pilate. Since Pilate can also be phonetically pronounced "pil-ot," it is another indirect reference to the theme of flying in the novel. Pilate soars beyond the effects of poverty. Other characters do not have that ability.

First Corinthians's name is also significant. It is taken from the name of a book of the Bible. Chapter thirteen offers insights into unconditional love. By picking this name, Morrison hints at Corinthians's pending love life.

Critical Response

Reviews for *Song of Solomon* were astounding. Among other tributes, the novel was a Book-of-the-Month Club main selection. This was a great honor. Morrison was the first African-American writer to be chosen for this honor since 1940, when Richard Wright's *Native Son* was the main selection. In 2006, the theater adaption of the novel debuted in New York City to mixed reviews.

MORE THAN A
GHOST TALE: *BELOVED*

Spirits, or ghosts, play prominent roles in many works of fiction. In *Beloved* the ghost is a central character, but the novel is much more than a ghost story designed to entertain or amuse readers. *Beloved* is a story about the continuing impact of slavery. Morrison depicts this legacy through the lives of former slaves. Morrison dedicated the novel to "Sixty Million and more," which refers to the estimated number of slaves who suffered and died in bondage. Morrison wrote the novel to recognize those slaves because:

> There is no place you or I can go, to think about or not think about, to summon the presences of, or recollect the absences of slaves; nothing that reminds us of the ones who made the journey and of those who did make it. There is no suitable memorial or plaque or wreath or wall or park or skyscraper lobby. There's no 300-foot tower. There's no small bench by the road. There is not even a tree scored, an initial that I can visit or you can visit in Charleston or Savannah or New York or Providence, or better still, on the banks of the Mississippi. And because such a place doesn't exist (that I know of), the book had to.[1]

The work shows the link between a person's past, present, and future. Sethe's memories and "rememories" illustrate that the past is almost a tangible part of the present, that there can be no future until the past, no matter how ugly and bloody, has been confronted squarely and placed securely in an appropriately constructive niche.[2]

Beloved is considered by many to be Morrison's finest work. Published in 1987, the novel won the Pulitzer Prize for Fiction one year later.

True to Life

Beloved is based on the true story of Margaret Garner. Garner was a runaway slave. She escaped from Kentucky to Ohio in 1856. She wanted to prevent her children from experiencing the horrors of slavery, but few options existed. When caught, Garner killed her three-year-old daughter. Garner's crime shocked the nation. People could not agree whether Garner was a cruel or loving mother.

The *Cincinnati Enquirer*'s original account of the story explains:

> The Abolitionists regard the parents of the murdered child as a hero and heroine, teeming with lofty and holy emotions, who, Virginiuslike would rather imbue their hands in the blood of their offspring than allow them to wear the shackles of slavery, while others look upon them as brutal and unnatural murderers.[3]

The issue was hotly debated. Lawmakers, politicians, and others looked at the case in light of the merits and drawbacks of slavery. One key issue was the definition of *slave*. Lawmakers had to determine if slaves were people or property. If they decided that slaves were people, Garner could be found guilty of murder. If they decided slaves were simply property, Garner's conviction would be limited to destruction of property.

Morrison is shown with a copy of *Beloved* in 1987, the year of its publication.

BENCH BY THE ROAD

When Toni Morrison wrote *Beloved* she felt there was no "bench by the road" to remember the slaves who died during slavery. That changed in 2006 when the Toni Morrison Society launched its "Bench by the Road" Project to celebrate Toni Morrison's seventy-fifth birthday. The project focuses on transforming the idea of a park bench into something much more. According to the society, its goal "is to create an outdoor museum that will mark important locations in African American history both in the United States and abroad."[4]

"Bench by the Road" locations include Delaware, Georgia, Massachusetts, Mississippi, New York, Ohio, Pennsylvania, South Carolina, and Washington, DC, as well as Paris, France, and Fort-de-France, Martinique. The Toni Morrison Society's website (www.tonimorrisonsociety .org) includes photographs of the Bench, a current list of locations, and each location's historic significance.

Those who favored slavery wanted this latter choice. They knew that if slaves were deemed people, many questions would be raised. One chief question would involve the poor treatment of slaves. In the end, Garner was charged with destroying property and returned to slavery.

Her case had lingering effects. It demonstrated Northern and Southern states' opposing views of slavery. Slavery was a chief cause of the Civil War, an intense four-year battle that began in February 1861 and ended in May 1865.

Abraham Lincoln was president of the United States at this time. During the war he issued the Emancipation Proclamation, the document that officially ended slavery. President Lincoln signed it on September 22, 1862, and it went into effect on January 1, 1863. Still, the war continued on for two more years. The Northern states won and emancipation prevailed.

Morrison draws from Margaret Garner's experiences to develop Sethe, the novel's main character. Sethe, like Garner, flees from Kentucky to Ohio. She, too, kills a baby daughter, preventing the child's return to slavery.

Morrison explains why she chose to write about the "daily struggle of slaves." She notes,

> I was trying to make it a personal experience. The book was not about the institution—Slavery with a capital S. It was about these anonymous people called slaves. What they do to keep on, how they make a life, what they're willing to risk, however long it lasts, in order to relate to one another—that was incredible to me.[5]

Themes

The legacy of slavery is the chief theme of *Beloved*. The novel shows how slaves suffered during and after slavery. Their

An illustration of Margaret Garner with her children and captors. Garner was a runaway slave who killed her child rather than have her returned to slavery. Morrison's *Beloved* was inspired by this story.

bodies, souls, and spirits were affected. Enacting legislation did not heal past trauma. Former slaves had to choose to leave their pasts behind.

Sethe and Paul D, for example, must confront past "ghosts" before they are fully free. These ghosts include hurts, fears, and coping mechanisms. Paul D is chief among those who react to circumstances by shutting down their emotions. His determination to only love a little bit falters when he reconnects with Sethe. Although loving Sethe is risky, Paul D meets the challenge.

Sethe, meanwhile, needs to overcome guilt stemming from her daughter Beloved's murder. Getting rid of that guilt opens the door for Sethe to enjoy a loving future with Paul D.

Not all characters rise above their slavery-related experiences. Lady Jones is one who does not. The light-skinned African-American woman suffers from identity issues related to her dual heritage. Morrison tells us:

> Lady Jones was mixed. Gray eyes and yellow wooly hair, every strand of which she hated—though whether it was the color or the texture even she didn't know. She had married the blackest man she could find, had five rainbow-colored children . . . She believed in her heart that, except for her husband, the whole world (including her children) despised her and her hair.[6]

Slavery's impact extends to the enslaving race. Stamp Paid muses:

> White people believed that whatever the manners, under each dark skin was a jungle . . . The more colored people spent their strength trying to convince them how gentle they were, how clever and loving, how human, the more they used themselves up to persuade whites of something Negroes believed could not be questioned, the

deeper and more tangled the jungle grew inside. But it wasn't the jungle blacks brought with them to this place from the other (livable) place. It was the jungle white folks planted in them. And it grew. It spread. In, through and after life, it spread, until it invaded the whites who had made it. Touched them every one. Changed and altered them. Made them bloody, silly, worse than even they wanted to be, so scared were they of the jungle they had made. The screaming baboon lived under their own white skin; the red gums were their own.[7]

Community Unity

Slave owners considered African Americans property, not people. They forced slaves to have children to increase the population, but slave families were usually split up. Children and parents could be sold at any time. As a result, slaves could not maintain the concept of family. African definitions of family were destroyed and American definitions denied to the slaves. Thus, understanding of community unity was limited. Emancipation changed that. Free African Americans could choose their spouses, raise their children, and stay connected with extended family members. Such opportunities astonished former slaves like Paul D.

> Once, in Maryland, he met four families of slaves who had all been together for a hundred years: great-grands, grands, mothers, fathers, aunts, uncles, cousins, children. Half white, part white, all black, mixed with Indian. He watched them with awe and envy, and each time he discovered large families of black people he made them identify over and over who each was, what relation, who, in fact, belonged to who.[8]

Beloved shows how unity is a key to family and community survival. The Underground Railroad succeeded mainly because people like Stamp Paid and Ella risked their lives to help strangers. Before discouragement steals her spiritual fervor and joy, Baby Suggs serves as a unifying force for the entire community. Likewise, Stamp Paid calls for community unity after learning no one had befriended or helped Paul D after he departed 124 Bluestone. When Stamp Paid mentions to Ella that he does not know where Paul D is, a heated discussion between the two begins:

> "He's sleeping in the church," said Ella.
> "The church!" Stamp was shocked and very hurt.
> "Yeah. Asked Reverend Pike if he could stay in the clear."
> "It's cold as charity in there!"
> "I expect he knows that."
> "What he do that for?"
> "He's a tough proud, seem like."
> "He don't have to do that! Any number'll take him in."
> Ella turned around to look at Stamp Paid. "Can't nobody read minds long distance. All he have to do is ask somebody."
> "Why, Why he have to ask? Can't nobody offer? What's going on? Since when a Blackman come to town have to sleep in a cellar like a dog?"
> "Unrile yourself, Stamp."
> "Not me. I'm going to stay riled till somebody gets some sense and leastway act like a Christian."[9]

Lack of community unity, fueled by jealousy over Baby Suggs's lavish party, enables the schoolteacher to reach Sethe without her knowledge of the pending threat of recapture. Residents do not sound an alarm, which may have provided ample opportunity for Sethe to escape. Had the community pulled together, events leading to Beloved's death may have turned out differently. But then unity resurfaces. Pulling together, community members provide food for Sethe's household, help Denver get a job, and exorcise Beloved.

Literary Devices

Symbolism is perhaps the most important literary device used in *Beloved*. Names, songs, and references to the Bible are all major symbols.

Symbolic names include Garner and Sweet Home. Garner is the surname of the owners of Sweet Home, the plantation central to the novel. Garner's name is the same as that of Margaret Garner, the slave whose story inspired Morrison's work. In *Beloved*, Mr. Garner is a softhearted slave owner who treats his slaves at Sweet Home plantation better than most slave owners treat them. Sweet Home slaves are neither whipped nor forced to have sexual relations just for the purpose of "breeding" more slaves. Females are assigned less strenuous tasks than males. The males, called Sweet Home men, openly share their thoughts and opinions with Mr. Garner and carry weapons to defend the plantation. Additionally, all Sweet Home slaves are allowed to marry, a situation neither generally accepted nor acknowledged at other plantations.

While Sweet Home slaves are treated better than other slaves on neighboring plantations, their names indicate that they are not viewed as individuals worthy of special names. Mr. Garner calls Baby Suggs "Jenny." He dubs Paul D and two other male slaves Paul, while identifying each by a letter of the alphabet. By so doing, Mr. Garner denies each man his individual identity. We never discover Beloved's name. She

103

In *Beloved*, the slaves on the Sweet Home plantation are treated better than most. Even so, Morrison shows how the slaves are stripped of their true identity.

chooses to call herself by the word inscribed on her tomb-stone. Barbara Hill Rigney contends:

> Sethe's name is one of the few in this novel chosen by a mother, and that name is a mark of blackness and acceptance into tribe and culture. As Nan tells the "small girl Sethe", "She threw them all away but you. The one from the crew, she threw away on the island. The others from more whites she also threw away. Without names, she threw them. You she gave the name of the black man . . ." Whether this name is derived from that of the Egyptian god Seth, or from the biblical Seth, it represents, like most of the names that Morrison designates as chosen, a sense of heritage and a context of relational identity.[10]

Slaves used songs to communicate secrets, plans, and other messages. Peter J. Capuano explains the use of songs in *Beloved*. He writes:

> Often in *Beloved* when characters cannot read or write or even talk about the brutality they experience as slaves, they sing to affirm their participation in life and defend their status as human beings. Song offers slaves the opportunity to express their personal testimonies while remaining within the framework of their larger cultural experiences—all without actually speaking of their shame and trauma.[11]

A Bible verse, Romans 9:25, is inscribed on the page after the dedication for *Beloved*. It reads, "I will call them my people, which were not my people; and her beloved which was not beloved."[12] Used in the context of this novel, that verse could symbolize the end of slavery or Beloved's reincarnation.

Other major symbols are trees, Paul D's heart, and colors. Trees are symbols of freedom, life, and peace. Paul D and the other Sweet Home men enjoy peace under the trees. Paul D later escapes to freedom by following different varieties of blooming trees. Trees populate the Clearing, where Baby Suggs holds her meetings.

Paul D's "tin tobacco" heart represents sealed emotions. He purposely tries to contain his feelings and experiences. The coping mechanism works until he reunites with Sethe. His relationship with her rips the lid off his emotions, making him recall and feel things he previously wished to forget. Once he opens himself up, however, Paul D is unable to stifle his feelings for Sethe. Thus, he is able to embrace a love-filled future.

Colors have several symbolic meanings. They represent racial differences, hope, and fear. When Baby Suggs retires to bed, she is defeated. She wants only to focus on bright colors, representative of hope, peace, and goodness. She is not willing to focus on black, which to her symbolizes death and bad happenings. Black also represents her oppressed race. Baby Suggs also does not want to see white. To her white represents the men who profited from slavery and oppressed African Americans. Baby Suggs chooses pink over red. In the novel red represents different things at different times. For Baby Suggs red represents blood and bloodshed, a reminder of Sethe's action. Beloved associates white with fear and calls white men "men without skin."

Plot Development

Sethe is a slave who flees to Ohio after responding to the call to escape. She heads to her mother-in-law's home. Baby Suggs has already welcomed Sethe's children. Sethe's escape is hindered by the fact that she is nine months pregnant. Bruised and exhausted, she falls down. A young white woman named Amy Denver finds Sethe. Amy encourages Sethe to crawl to a nearby shelter. Once there, Amy takes care of Sethe's aching feet and later provides help as Sethe delivers a baby girl. The two women separate the next day and never see each other again.

The novel begins eighteen years after Sethe arrives in Ohio. She and her daughter Denver reside alone in Baby Suggs's home at 124 Bluestone Road, along with a ghost named Beloved who most believe is Sethe's dead child. Baby Suggs died eight years earlier. Years before, Sethe's sons, spooked by the haunted house, had run away. Sethe's and Denver's decision to remain in the haunted house results in their isolation from the community. Residents also shun the family because they are outraged that Sethe killed her baby daughter rather than return her to a life of slavery.

That isolation is shattered upon the arrival of Paul D, a former Sweet Home slave and Sethe's friend. Paul D has not seen Sethe in eighteen years. As their relationship develops, so does the strife within the home.

Denver is unhappy about this new relationship for two reasons. First, Beloved is her only friend, and Paul D has chased the ghost from the house. Second, Paul D monopolizes her mother's affection, which Denver wants but is afraid to seek. Ever since Sethe murdered Beloved, Denver has been afraid of her mother.

Shortly after Beloved is banned from the house, she reappears in the form of a woman. Sethe invites her into the home. That decision opens the door for Beloved to begin a different type of haunting.

> Sethe was flattered by Beloved's open, quiet devotion. The same adoration from her daughter (had it been forthcoming) would have annoyed her; made her chill at the thought of having raised a ridiculously dependent

child. But the company of this sweet, if peculiar, guest pleased her the way a zealot pleases his teacher.[13]

Paul D is less enamored with Beloved.

> He wanted her out, but Sethe had let her in and he couldn't put her out of a house that wasn't his. It was one thing to beat up a ghost, quite another to throw a helpless colored girl out in territory infected by the Klan.[14]

Beloved's obsessive behavior and the truth concerning her death cause Paul D to leave 124 Bluestone. His departure opens the door for a more intense, yet harmful, relationship between Sethe and Beloved. Once Sethe realizes that Beloved is her long-dead daughter, she is elated. That elation does not last, as the two women develop a strange dependency upon each other.

Watching the situation evolve, Denver determines to help. She steps out of her home and into the community for the first time in more than a decade.

Once the women in the community hear that Beloved has returned from the dead and is taunting Sethe, they take action. Ultimately, thirty women are responsible for exorcising Beloved from 124 Bluestone and the community. Beloved disappears. She does not return.

Sethe is overcome by the events. Despite Beloved's poisonous nature, Sethe considered Beloved "my best thing." Grief-stricken, Sethe moves into Baby Suggs's bed. She prepares to die in a similar fashion. Her plan is thwarted by Paul D. "Sethe," he says, "me and you, we got more yesterday than anybody. We need some kind of tomorrow."[15]

Several characters in *Beloved* play a role in the Underground Railroad, a network formed by abolitionists who wanted to help free the slaves.

Character Development

Morrison illustrates the legacy of slavery through the lives of six essential characters: Sethe, Denver, Beloved, Paul D, Baby Suggs, and Stamp Paid.

Sethe

Pretty, young Sethe arrives at Sweet Home at age thirteen. Her beauty and availability cause the Sweet Home men to fantasize about her. They do not force themselves upon Sethe, but await her selection. Halle's devotion to his mother, as demonstrated by his working extra days to buy her freedom, impresses Sethe. After a year Sethe finally selects him. They marry and have three children—two boys, Howard and Buglar, and a daughter, whose actual name is never mentioned.

Despite being allowed to purchase his mother's freedom, Halle never buys into the idea that Mr. Garner is a benevolent slave owner who truly cares about the Sweet Home slaves. Halle's offer to work additional hours to earn money for his mother's freedom backfires when the new master, known as schoolteacher, takes over the plantation. No longer allowed to work outside of Sweet Home and restricted in other ways, Halle resigns himself to never being able to pay for his and his family's freedom. Agreeing to an escape plan plotted with the other Sweet Home men, Halle fails to run away in time. Instead, he goes insane after witnessing schoolteacher's nephews physically assault Sethe, stealing her breast milk.

Sethe is pregnant with their fourth child when she escapes to Cincinnati, Ohio, to live with her mother-in-law. Howard and Buglar, sent ahead, are awaiting Sethe, who arrives safely at Baby Suggs's home. For twenty-eight glorious days Sethe enjoys freedom and the luxury of loving her children and living in a community of free African Americans.

That joy is short-circuited when schoolteacher discovers her whereabouts. He and three other gun-toting white men arrive at Baby Suggs's intent on bringing Sethe and her children back to slavery. Sethe, however, is as adamant that her children never experience the life she did. The only way to prevent that, she believes, is to kill herself and her children. She succeeds in killing the child who becomes known after death as Beloved. Sethe spends a short time in prison and later lives the rest of her life at Baby Suggs's house.

Sethe's life is plagued by memories of slavery. She cannot completely forget the atrocities she experienced or feel secure enough to love someone else. In order for Sethe to remain free from Beloved, who first haunts the house, then returns from the dead as a young woman, Sethe must relinquish past hurts and regrets.

Paul D

Paul D, one of the Sweet Home men, finds life as a slave endurable until the plantation comes under the control of a new master. Emotionally crushed by the abuse he suffers and other slavery-related incidents, Paul D survives with a "tin tobacco" heart, his term for badly bruised emotions. Ultimately, Paul D escapes from Kentucky. He moves from place to place until finding Sethe in Cincinnati. Paul D never expected to begin a romantic relationship with her or to move in. But he does both.

Initially, he stays only a few months. One of the reasons is the guilt and shame he feels for entering into a sexual relationship with Beloved. Another is that Paul D finally discovers that Sethe hurt her children. He is shocked and disgusted, noting, "What you did was wrong, Sethe."[16] He cannot understand how a mother's protective instinct could make her harm her children. In his mind only an animal would do so. "'You got two feet, not four,' he said, and right then a forest sprang up between them; trackless and quiet."[17]

Eventually Paul D returns to Sethe. Beloved has disappeared, Denver is more welcoming, but Sethe appears ready to die. Upon seeing her, Paul D commits to love and take care of her. Paul D's reaction reveals his character development. Wilfred D. Samuel and Clenora Hudson-Weems write,

> [Paul's D's] sense of fulfillment comes from within, as his advice to Sethe clearly implies; for he, too, must have reached the realization that he is his own best thing before he could attempt to pass it on. Paul D is finally able to look at Sethe on more than a superficial level. Seeing her for the first time with a more authentic perspective, he comes to accept her as a friend of his mind.[18]

Denver

Denver, the youngest of Sethe's children, is the only child who gets to live with Sethe from infancy through adulthood. An immature young woman, Denver fears venturing outside of her home, mainly because she has been isolated for years from other people.

Ironically, Beloved's arrival makes it possible for Denver to experience life. For most of her life, Denver is a lonely, dependent person who it appears will never have a hope of living normally. She only learns self-sufficiency after seeking help from the community. She thinks, "Somebody had to be saved, but unless Denver got work, there would be no one to save, no one to come home to, and no Denver either." For Denver, "It was a new thought, having a self to look out for and preserve."[19]

At the end of the novel, it is clear that Denver has experienced a complete emotional and mental transformation.

Beloved

By all evidence, Beloved is Sethe's oldest daughter. Her character is an example of Morrison's ambiguity because we never truly learn who Beloved is. Sethe considers murdering her infant daughter the ultimate act of love and sacrifice. To Beloved it is an act of rejection. Thus, the spiteful ghost of Beloved haunts 124 Bluestone Road until Paul D throws her spirit out of the home.

Beloved reappears as a woman. At least it seems as if the stranger is Sethe's daughter. Her identity is ambiguous; Morrison never clearly tells us who she is.

Beloved is childlike. At first, she seems sweet and loving. After a while, she demands Sethe's complete love, affection, and acceptance. Beloved becomes increasingly obsessed with Sethe and Sethe's past. Possessive and vindictive, she tries to isolate Sethe from everyone else. Beloved's hold on Sethe is broken when the community women visit 124 Bluestone. Seeking God's help, they pray and sing. It is not clear what causes Beloved to disappear; perhaps it is the women's actions or maybe Sethe's anger. Whatever the reason, Beloved is gone. Focusing on the present breaks any future hold Beloved may have.

Baby Suggs

Baby Suggs is a free African-American woman. Her son, Halle, buys her freedom by working extra hours. Once free, she relocates to Cincinnati. Two abolitionists help Baby Suggs get a job and provide a house for her to live in. Her home quickly becomes a central meeting place.

> Before 124 and everybody in it had closed down, veiled
> over and shut away; before it had become the plaything
> of spirits and the home of the chafed, 124 had been a
> cheerful, buzzing house where Baby Suggs, holy, loved,
> cautioned, fed, chastised and soothed. Where not one
> but two pots simmered on the stove; where the lamp
> burned all night long. Strangers rested there while
> children tried on their shoes. Messages were left there,
> for whoever needed them was sure to stop in one day
> soon.[20]

Baby Suggs also becomes a spiritual leader to her community. She helps them stay unified.

> Accepting no title of honor before her name, but allowing
> a small caress after it, she became an unchurched
> preacher, one who visited pulpits and opened her great
> heart to those who could use it . . . When warm weather
> came, Baby Suggs, holy, followed by every black man,
> woman and child who could make it through, took her
> great heart to the Clearing—a wide-open place cut deep
> in the woods nobody knew for what at the end of a path
> known only to deer and whoever cleared the land in the
> first place. In the heat of every Saturday afternoon, she
> sat in the clearing while the people awaited among the
> trees.[21]

Baby Suggs offers fun and laughter. She allows time for men, women, and children to renew their spirits and souls. She changes after Beloved's death. "Her faith, her love, her imagination and her great big old heart began to collapse twenty-eight days after her daughter-in-law arrived."[22]

Upset by the killing, the community shuns Baby Suggs and her family. Over time, only Stamp Paid continues to befriend them. Baby Suggs is heartbroken, refusing to get out of her bed. She stops leading the meeting at the Clearing. She spends time focusing on colors, which symbolizes her desire for nonthreatening activities. She prefers blue, yellow, and pink. Baby Suggs ignores white, which represents white people and their deeds.

Stamp Paid

Ferrying slaves to freedom is a joy for Stamp Paid, a conductor for the Underground Railroad. He changes his name from Joshua to Stamp Paid to reflect the fact that he believes any debt he owed to society is fully paid. Stamp Paid feels he paid the ultimate price when he "handed over his wife to his master's son."[23] Barbara Rigney says that Stamp Paid's name "represents a rejection of a tradition of white naming as well as a celebration of freedom."[24]

Although his wife returns, Stamp Paid escapes to freedom, later becoming a critical link in the Underground Railroad system. The Underground Railroad was a secretive network of white abolitionists, free African Americans, and former slaves who helped slaves escape from slavery. Members of the network risked their lives providing food, shelter, and other aid to slaves escaping from Southern states to free Northern states.

Because of his activities, Stamp is one of the town's saviors. Well-liked and influential, Stamp is the only community member concerned about events at 124 Bluestone Road.

Ella

Ella cannot forget the devastating sexual assault she experiences at the hands of a white father and son, "whom she called 'the lowest yet.' It was the 'lowest yet' who gave her a disgust for sex and against whom she measured all atrocities."[25] From that

Morrison receives the Nobel Prize in Literature from King Carl XVI Gustaf of Sweden in 1993. She was the first African-American woman to receive the prestigious prize.

point onward, Ella has an aversion to all love, not just romantic relationships. Nobody loves her and she would not have liked it if they had, for she considers love a serious disability.[26] Ella's inability to love others illustrates how a person's past negatively affects all future relationships.

Ella is involved in the Underground Railroad. She assists when Sethe originally comes to town. But Sethe's murder of Beloved ultimately causes Ella to distance herself from the family. She understands Sethe's rage in the shed twenty years ago, but not the way she reacts to it, which Ella thinks was prideful and misdirected.[27]

Despite her feelings, Ella steps in to help rid 124 Bluestone of Beloved. She organizes a band of women rescuers because

> [w]hatever Sethe had done, Ella didn't like the idea of past errors taking possession of the present. Sethe's crime was staggering and her pride outstripped even that; but she could not countenance the possibility of sin moving on in the house, unleashed and sassy. Daily life took as much as she had. The future was sunset; the past something to leave behind. And if it didn't stay behind, well, you might have to stomp it out.[28]

Schoolteacher

Schoolteacher takes over Sweet Home plantation after Mr. Garner dies. The coldhearted, cruel overseer transforms Sweet Home into a place of despair and fear, from which the slaves flee. He systematically begins a series of reforms that radically alters slaves' lives. Unlike Mr. Garner, schoolteacher rules by force, viciously implementing rules and regulations that shatter the slaves' bodies, minds, and spirits. He adopts a demeaning scientific approach to handling the slaves, treating them like property and viewing them as animals. Morrison uses irony in naming the plantation, which is a place of bondage.

Mr. and Mrs. Garner

Mr. and Mrs. Garner own Sweet Home plantation. They believe they are morally better than their peers because Sweet Home slaves are treated with kindness and respect. Ultimately, however, their actions prove detrimental, as Sweet Home slaves are unable to handle the realities of slavery that exist outside of the Garners' plantation—and thus protection. Morrison's use of irony is further seen in the development of the Garners. The couple treats the slaves as if they are special, but at the same time makes it difficult for them to adjust to the real rigors of slavery.

Rants and Raves

Reviews for *Beloved* were positive. Walter Clemons wrote, "At the heart of this astounding book, prose narrative dissolves into a hypnotic, poetic conversation among Sethe, Denver, and the otherworldly Beloved."[29] Other reviewers criticized the reincarnation theme. Yet Morrison thought it was appropriate given the era she wrote about.

Beloved's fame soared. In 1988, Morrison was awarded the Pulitzer Prize in Literature for the novel. Ten years later the movie version of the novel debuted. *Beloved* starred a cast of famous African-American actors. Talk show host Oprah Winfrey played Sethe. Some critics, such as Scott Galupo, felt the movie was horrible. In a *Washington Times* article he called it a "dismal film."[30]

A writer for *Variety* called it a "neutron bomb," suggesting that though it did not destroy the studio that produced it, it effectively killed the careers of many of those involved.[31]

Despite such negative criticism of the film adaptation, Morrison's status grew.

Beloved's popularity continued to grow many years after its release. In 2008 the *New York Times* named *Beloved* as the "Best Work of American Fiction of the Last 25 Years."

The Dancing Mind:
Toni Morrison Today

Imagine having your book turned into a feature film. People in many cities and states can go to the theater and watch your work unfold. That is what happened when *Beloved* was released in 1998. Most authors never see their work on film. Authors whose books do appear on film often experience renewed interest in their work. The movie version sparked increased interest in *Beloved*, specifically, and other works by Morrison, generally.

As Seen on Oprah

It was not surprising that Oprah Winfrey appeared in *Beloved*. Winfrey often talks about how much she loves Morrison's fiction. She has also named several of Morrison's books as Oprah's Book Club selections. The book club was a special feature of her television show before its final episode in 2011. Each time Winfrey chose a book, she encouraged viewers to buy it. Authors, such as Morrison, later appeared on the show. Sometimes they discussed their works. Other times they had an opportunity to read from one of their works.

Book sales increased whenever Winfrey announced her Oprah's Book Club choice. John Young argues:

Morrison is joined by Oprah Winfrey at the film premiere for *Beloved* in 1998. Winfrey's support of the writer on her television program helped significantly increase Morrison's readership.

Before her first Oprah appearance in December, 1996, Morrison was a Nobel and Pulitzer Prize winner, an endowed professor at Princeton University, and one of the most respected voices in contemporary American literature ... [S]ince aligning herself with Winfrey, Morrison has become the best-selling author of *Song of Solomon*, nineteen years after its first publication; of *Paradise* ... probably the least accessible book she has yet written; and of *The Bluest Eye*.[1]

Retired Educator

One year after winning the Pulitzer, Morrison received a key appointment. She was named the Robert F. Goheen Professor in the Humanities at Princeton University. She retired in 2006. In 2014 the university announced Morrison's papers would be held at the university. An author's papers often include drafts of his or her books and other things important to the writing. Morrison's papers, for example, include drafts of *The Bluest Eye*.

Recent Works

Morrison's more recent works include *A Mercy* (2008), *Home* (2012), and *God Help the Child* (2015). *God Help the Child* had readers again applauding Morrison's creative genius in addition to her courage in writing about tough topics. Child abuse is a key theme in the novel.

In her book review in the *New York Times* Kara Walker notes:

Child abuse cuts a jagged scar through Toni Morrison's "God Help the Child," a brisk modern-day fairy tale with shades of the Brothers Grimm: imaginative cruelties visited on children; a journey into the woods; a handsome, vanished lover; witchy older women and a blunt moral—"What you do to children matters. And they might never forget."[2]

Morrison's other novels include *Jazz* (1992), *Paradise* (1998), and *Love* (2003). She also has recorded audiobook versions of her novels.

In addition to her novels, Morrison has penned plays. *Desdemona*, a play based on Shakespeare's *Othello*, opened in 2011. Another of her plays is *Dreaming Emmett*, a play based on the murder of Emmett Till. The play debuted in Albany, New York, in 1986.

Another new project of Morrison's involves children's books. Her books did not draw immediate interest. Some publishers doubted if she would make a good children's book author. They also wondered if readers would accept Morrison's entry into a new genre. Morrison kept trying.

> **genre**
>
> A class of literary works that usually shares a common content or style.

Her diligence was rewarded when a publisher gave her a contract. The first book, coauthored with her son Slade, was released in 1999.[3] It is a rhyming picture book entitled *The Big Box*. The second, *The Book of Mean People*, also a picture book, was published in 2002. Morrison next developed with Slade the Who's Got Game? series. Books in the series include the 2003 releases *The Ant or the Grasshopper?* and *The Lion or the Mouse?* Another book, *Poppy or the Snake?* came out in 2004. Mother and son collaborated on other projects before Slade died in 2010 from pancreatic cancer.

Morrison's first historical children's book, *Remember: The Journey to School Integration*, was published in 2004.

Over the years, Morrison has received numerous honorary degrees from colleges and universities. Here she speaks to graduates after receiving an honorary degree from Rutgers University in 2011.

It recalls the road to school integration in the United States. It includes photographs and fictional dialogue of children who lived during the times when schools were being integrated. The book garnered Morrison the 2005 Coretta Scott King Award. That award, presented by the American Library Association, honors "African American authors and illustrators of outstanding books for children and young adults."

In addition to these projects, Morrison penned *Margaret Garner*, an opera based on the slave whose story inspired *Beloved*. The opera's world debut was held at the Detroit Opera House in early 2005.

Impact on African-American Literature

Two factors are key to Morrison's lasting impact on African-American literature: her job as an editor and the popularity of her own books.

Morrison helped many aspiring writers when she was an editor. Dinita Smith, writing in the *New York Times*, notes that "[at] Random House [Morrison] nurtured black authors who became staples of African-American literature—Angela Davis, June Jordan, Wesley Brown, and Toni Cade Bambara. She also edited *The Black Book*, an anthology of black history."[4]

Morrison's own writing fed readers' appetites for works by black authors. Trudier Harris states, "In the best of worlds, Morrison's success could open doors for young writers following after her, something that she had indicated in interviews is important to her."[5]

Enduring Legacy

One of the most exciting projects that will keep Morrison's legacy alive is the Bench by the Road project. This project has national and international appeal and impact. The society

Remembering Emmett Till

Morrison based her play *Dreaming Emmett* on the true story of Emmett Till. The African-American teenager from Chicago was killed in August 1955 while visiting relatives in Money, Mississippi. He was fourteen years old when he died. Many people credit his death with sparking the civil rights movement in the United States.

Before leaving a local store, Till allegedly whistled at a white woman. That act was considered disrespectful and insulting. Later that evening a group of white men visited his uncle's home. They demanded that Till come out. They tortured and killed him. He was first beaten and then shot. The crime drew national attention after his mother demanded his body be flown back home, then allowed it to be viewed at the funeral.

> Approximately 50,000 people, nearly all of them black, turned out for Till's funeral, in an enormous public display of grief and solidarity. Mamie Till ordered the funeral director to place her son in an open casket, and permitted a shocking photograph of Till's corpse to be published in *Jet* magazine and seen across the country. This ignited protests, civil disobedience and a backlash that would consume the South through the sixties.[6]

Two men, relatives of the woman Till supposedly insulted, were tried for kidnapping and murder. They were acquitted. One of the men later admitted to a reporter that he had participated in the murder. Despite this, over the years there have been unsuccessful attempts to solve Till's murder.

At the time Morrison penned *Dreaming Emmett*, which opened in 1986, Till's murder was still unsolved.

In the play, Till comes back from the grave to torment

the men and women responsible for his death. By the end of the play, however, the audience learns that the boy is not Emmett Till at all, but another boy who was shot in the back by a white Chicago storekeeper for stealing a kite. "Everyone knows Emmett," he explains, while he is anonymous. He assumed Till's identity so someone would remember he existed.[7]

Six years after Morrison's play debuted, Emmett Till's murder was reinvestigated. On May 11, 2004, the US Justice Department announced it was reopening the case. According to a 60 *Minutes* report, the new investigation was "based on evidence suggesting that more than a dozen people may have been involved in the murder of Till, and that at least five of them were still alive."[8]

Emmett Till is seen here in a photo that adorns his gravestone plaque in Aslip, Illinois. The black teenager was brutally murdered by several white men in 1955. Till's story was later the basis for Morrison's play, *Dreaming Emmett*.

Morrison attends a ceremony in Paris, France, to unveil a bench as part of the Bench by the Road project. The project was started as a way to remember the lives of the slaves. The Toni Morrison Society plans to dedicate at least twenty of the benches in sites that have special significance for African Americans.

notes, "Our hope is that the Bench by the Road Project will serve not only to acknowledge Toni Morrison's attention to these historic sites and their meanings in her novels but also to mark their locations, inspire dialogue, and engage them as part of our public memory."[9]

Beyond these markers, every year, new readers, including high school and college students, discover her work. Moreover, thanks to technological advances such as ebooks and audiobooks, Morrison's works are more accessible than ever.

Technology is but one means by which Morrison's legacy is growing. Global efforts also play a role. Her hometown library in Lorain, Ohio, opened a reading room in her honor. The Toni Morrison Society, started in 1998, hosts events and activities related to her writings. The society also sponsors workshops for high school teachers who want to teach Morrison's works.

Morrison's legacy is guaranteed:

> Toni Morrison stands in the vanguard of contemporary writers of fiction . . . her success as a writer transcends both her racial identity and gender. She is not only a leading African-American woman novelist, though this is most noteworthy, she is one of the most significant and relevant writers on the literary scene today. Her acclaim is international . . . Scholars and doctoral candidates the world over critique and assess her works, seeking to unravel the complexity that Morrison prides.[10]

As Ann Geracimos aptly notes, "[Her] life is the stuff of which legends are made, beginning with her childhood growing up poor but proud in the blue-collar town of Lorain, Ohio, where she had a job cleaning houses after school."[11]

Her acclaim should not surprise anyone visiting Morrison's magical world of fiction. After all, in her world anything can, and does, happen.

CHRONOLOGY

1931—Chloe Anthony Wofford is born on February 18 in Lorain, Ohio.

1949—Graduates with honors from Lorain High School.

1949—Attends Howard University in Washington, DC; begins to use the name "Toni."

1953—Graduates from Howard University with degree in English.

1955—Graduates from Cornell University in Ithaca, New York, with a master of arts degree in English.

1955–1957—Teaches at Texas Southern University in Houston, Texas.

1957—Begins teaching at Howard University.

1958—Marries Harold Morrison.

1961—Gives birth to first son, Harold Ford.

1964—Marriage ends; returns home to Lorain, Ohio; son Slade Kevin is born.

1965—Moves to Syracuse, New York, for editing job at Random House publishing company.

1967—Moves to New York City to work as senior editor in Random House's headquarters.

1970—Publishes first novel, *The Bluest Eye*.

1971–1972—Works as an associate professor at the State University of New York in Purchase, New York.

1973—Publishes *Sula*.

1974—*The Black Book*, edited by Morrison, is published.

1975—*Sula* is nominated for National Book Award for fiction.

1976–1997—Becomes visiting lecturer at Yale University.

1977—Publishes *Song of Solomon*. It wins two awards: American Academy and Institute of Arts and Letters Award and the National Book Critics Circle Award;

President Carter names her to National Council on the Arts.

1981—*Tar Baby* is published.

1983—Morrison ends twenty-year career with Random House.

1984—Works as a professor at the State University of New York at Albany.

1986—Play *Dreaming Emmett* opens in Albany.

1987—Publishes *Beloved*.

1988—Receives the Pulitzer Prize in fiction for *Beloved*.

1989–Present—Leads Princeton University's Humanities department; makes history as first African American to hold such a position at an Ivy League college.

1990—Receives Chianti Ruffino Antico Fattore International Literary Prize.

1992—Releases *Jazz*; publishes *Playing in the Dark: Whiteness and the Literary Imagination*, a book of essays.

1993—Becomes first black woman to receive the Nobel Prize in Literature; the Toni Morrison Society is established.

1995—Receives Matrix Awards (book category); gets honorary Doctor of Humane Letters from Howard University.

1996—Releases *The Dancing Mind*.

1998—Releases *Beloved* the movie; publishes *Paradise*.

1999—Publishes *The Big Box*, a children's book coauthored with son Slade.

2000—Releases audiobook of *The Bluest Eye*; Library of Congress names Morrison a "Living Legend."

2002—Oprah Winfrey's Book Club features *Sula*; *The Book of Mean People* debuts.

2003—Publishes *Love*; releases *The Ant or the Grasshopper?*

and *The Lion or the Mouse?*

2004—Publishes *The Poppy or the Snake?* in the Who's Got Game? series; releases *Remember: The Journey to School Integration*; receives NAACP Image Award for Outstanding Literary Work–Fiction for *Love.*

2005—*Margaret Garner* opera debuts; wins Coretta Scott King Award for *Remember: The Journey to School Integration*; publishes *The Mirror or the Glass?*

2006—The *New York Times* names *Beloved* as the "Best Work of American Fiction of the Last 25 Years"; Morrison retires from Princeton University.

2008—Releases *A Mercy;* Toni Morrison Society dedicates first Bench by the Road, placed in Sullivan's Island, South Carolina.

2009—Serves as editor of *Burn This Book: PEN Writers Speak Out on the Power of the Word*; releases *Peeny Butter Fudge.*

2010—Releases *Little Cloud and Lady Wind.*

2011—Receives the National Book Festival Creative Achievement Award; *Desdemona* play opens in France.

2012—Receives President Medal of Freedom; publishes *Home.*

2013—Receives New York City Literary Honors for Fiction.

2014—Princeton University announces the papers of Toni Morrison will be housed at the university; publishes *Please, Louise.*

2015—Releases *God Help the Child.*

CHAPTER NOTES

Chapter 1. Presidential Honor

1. The White House, Press Release, "Remarks by the President at Presidential Medal of Freedom Ceremony," May 29, 2012, https://www.whitehouse.gov/the-press-office/2012/05/29/remarks-president-presidential-medal-freedom-ceremony.
2. Ibid.
3. The White House, Press Release, "President Obama Names Presidential Medal of Freedom Recipients," April 26, 2012, https://www.whitehouse.gov/the-press-office/2012/04/26/president-obama-names-presidential-medal-freedom-recipients.
4. Rachel Kaadzi Ghansah, "The Radical Vision of Toni Morrison," *New York Times*, April 8, 2015, http://www.nytimes.com/2015/04/12/magazine/the-radical-vision-of-toni-morrison.html?_r=0.
5. Penguin Group, "The Books of Toni Morrison," *Penguin Putnam Reading Guides,* http://www.penguinputnam.com/static/rguides/us/toni_morrison.html (accessed May 14, 2004).
6. *Encyclopedia.com*, "Harlem Renaissance," http://www.encyclopedia.com/html/h/harlemr1en.asp (accessed May 16, 2005).
7. Beth Rowen and Borgna Brunner, "Great Days in Harlem: The Birth of the Harlem Renaissance," *Infoplease*, http://www.infoplease.com/spot/bhmharlem1.html (accessed May 16, 2005).
8. *Encyclopedia.com*, "Harlem Renaissance."
9. Ibid.
10. Ibid.

11. Toni Morrison, transcript of January 21, 1998, online chat, http://www.time.com/time/community/transcripts/chattr012198.html.
12. Penguin Group, "The Books of Toni Morrison."
13. Zia Jaffrey, "The *Salon* interview—Toni Morrison," Salon, February 2, 1998, http://dir.salon.com/books/int/1998/02/02/cov_si_02int/index.html?pn=1.
14. "Toni Morrison's Gift," *Boston Globe*, October 8, 1993, 22.
15. Toni Morrison, *Song of Solomon* (New York: Plume, 1987), p. 337.
16. Barbara Hill Rigney, *The Voices of Toni Morrison* (Columbus, OH: Ohio State University Press, 1991), p. 8.
17. Toni Morrison, *The Bluest Eye* (New York: Plume, 1994), p. 58.
18. Barbara Christian, *Black Feminist Criticism* (New York: Teachers College Press, 1991), p. 47.
19. Wilfred D. Samuels and Clenora Hudson-Weems, *Toni Morrison* (Boston: Twayne Publishers, 1990), p. x.
20. Christian, p. 79.
21. Kathy Sun, "Morrison Discusses Her Novels and Shares Her Ideas," *Tech* 112, no. 24, (May 1, 1992): 12, http://www-tech.mit.edu/V112/N24/morrison.24a.html.
22. Trudier Harris, "Toni Morrison: Solo Flight Through Literature into History," *World Literature Today* 68, no.1, (1994): 9–14, http://www.questia.com.

Chapter 2. Pioneering Author

1. Stephanie Li, *Toni Morrison: A Biography* (California: Greenwood Press, 2010), p. 31.
2. Rachel Kaadzi Ghansah, "The Radical Vision of Toni Morrison." *New York Times*, April 8, 2015, http://www.

nytimes.com/2015/04/12/magazine/the-radical-vision-of-toni-morrison.html?_r=0.

3. Denise Heinze, *The Dilemma of "Double-Consciousness"* (Athens: University of Georgia Press, 1993), p. 3.

4. Li, p. xiii.

5. Penguin Group, "The Books of Toni Morrison," *Penguin Putnam Reading Guides*, http://www.penguinputnam.com/static/rguides/us/toni_morrison.html (accessed May 14, 2004).

6. Ghansah.

7. Trudier Harris, "Toni Morrison: Solo Flight Through Literature into History," *World Literature Today* 68, no. 1, (1994): 9–14, http://www.questia.com.

8. Bonnie Angelo, "The Pain of Being Black," *Time*, May 22, 1989, http://www.time.com/time/community/pulitizerinterview.html.

9. Ibid.

10. Ibid.

11. Penguin Group, "The Books of Toni Morrison."

12. Barbara Hill Rigney, *The Voices of Toni Morrison* (Columbus, OH: Ohio State University Press, 1991), p. 44.

13. Li, p. 52

14. Toni Morrison, *The Bluest Eye* (New York: Plume, 1994), p. 46.

15. "Best 100 Characters in Fiction Since 1900," *Book Magazine*, March–April 2002, 38, http://www.questia.com.

16. Toni Morrison, *Song of Solomon* (New York: Plume, 1994), p. 323.

17. Ibid., p. 128.

18. Toni Morrison, *Beloved* (New York: Plume, 1988), p. 3.

19. Ibid., p. 275.

20. Morrison, *The Bluest Eye*, p. 13.

21. Adam Langer, "*Love* is Toni Morrison's Best Novel in More than a Decade. Now She's Aiming Even Higher," *Book Magazine*, November–December 2003, http://www.questia. com.

22. Barbara Christian, *Black Feminist Criticism* (New York: Teachers College Press, 1991), p. 172.

23. Ibid., p. 17.

24. Rigney, p. 36.

25. Marla W. Iyasere and Solomon O. Iyasere, eds., *Understanding Toni Morrison's* Beloved *and* Sula: *Selected Essays and Criticisms of the Works by the Nobel Prize– Winning Author* (Troy, NY: Whitston Publishing, 2000), p. xiv.

26. Karen Carmean, *Toni Morrison's World of Fiction* (Troy, NY: Whitston Publishing, 1993), p. 15.

27. Maria Lauret, contributor, *Liberating Literature: Feminist Fiction in America* (New York: Routledge, 1994), p. 142.

28. Zia Jaffrey, "The *Salon* Interview—Toni Morrison," *Salon*, February 2, 1998, http://dir.salon.com/books/ int/1998/02/02/cov_si_02int/index.html?pn=1.

29. Ibid.

Chapter 3. Creative Genius

1. Roxanne Gay, "The Hemi Q&A: Toni Morrison." *Hemispheres*, http://www.hemispheresmagazine. com/2015/05/01/the-hemi-qa-toni-morrison/ (accessed July 29, 2015).

2. Lisa Clayton Robinson, "Toni Morrison," *Encarta Africana*, http://www.africana.research/encarta/tt_196.asp (accessed May 16, 2005).

3. Toni Morrison, *Beloved* (New York: Plume, 1988), p. 58.

4. Danuta Bois, "Toni Morrison," *Distinguished Women of Past and Present: Toni Morrison,* 1996, http://www. distinguishedwomen.com/biographies/morrison.html.

5. Trudier Harris, "Toni Morrison: Solo Flight Through Literature into History," *World Literature Today* 68, no. 1, (1994): 9–14, http://www.questia.com.

6. Penguin Putnam, "The Books of Toni Morrison," *Penguin Putnam Reading Guides,* http://www.penguinputnam.com/ static/rguides/us/toni_morrison.html (accessed May 14, 2004).

7. Harris.

8. "White House Announces the 2000 National Humanities Medalists," *National Endowment for the Humanities,* December 15, 2000, http://www.neh.gov/news/archive/ 20001215.html.

9. Penguin Putnam, "The Books of Toni Morrison."

10. Ann Geracimos, "Writer Toni Morrison through the Eyes of Friends: Always a Champion of Language," *Washington Times,* March 24, 1996, 3, http://www.questia.com.

11. Elizabeth Farnsworth, "Conversation: Toni Morrison," *The NewsHour with Jim Lehrer Transcript,* March 9, 1998, http:// www.pbs.org/newshour/bb/entertainment/jan-june98/ morrison_3-9.html.

12. Ibid.

13. Harris.

14. "Faulkner, William," *The Columbia Encyclopedia,* 6th ed., http://www.questia.com (accessed May 11, 2004).

15. Barbara Christian, *Black Feminist Criticism* (New York: Teachers College Press, 1991), p. 48.

16. "The South" *The Columbia Encyclopedia,* 6th ed. (New York: Columbia University Press, 2001–04), http://www. bartleby.com/65/.

17. Harris.

Chapter 4. Reclaiming Racial Beauty

1. Elissa Schappel, "Toni Morrison, The Art of Fiction No. 134," *Paris Review*, Fall 1993.
2. Karen Carmean, *Toni Morrison's World of Fiction* (Troy, NY: Whitston, 1993), p. 19.
3. Toni Morrison, *The Bluest Eye* (New York: Plume, 1994), pp. 210–211.
4. Valerie Boyd, "Black and Blue: An Unforgettable Literary Debut, *The Bluest Eye* Was Toni Morrison's Attempt to Expel the Despair of a Generation," *Book Magazine*, January–February 2003, 27, http://www.questia.com.
5. Ibid.
6. Morrison, p. 209.
7. Barbara Christian, *Black Feminist Criticism* (New York: Teachers College Press, 1991), p. 48.
8. Ibid., pp. 48–49.
9. Morrison, p. 118.
10. Cornell West, *Race Matters* (Boston: Beacon Press, 1993), p. 18.
11. Boyd.
12. Ibid.
13. Morrison, p. 210.
14. Ibid., p. 19.
15. Ibid., p. 38.
16. Ibid., p. 39.
17. Ibid., pp. 38–39.
18. Robert Sargent, "A Way of Ordering Experience: A Study of Toni Morrison's *The Bluest Eye* and *Sula*," *Faith of a (Woman) Writer*, eds. Alice Kessler-Harris and William McBrien (New York: Greenwood Press, 1988), p. 231.

19. Ibid., p. 234.
20. Trudier Harris, "Toni Morrison: Solo Flight Through Literature into History," *World Literature Today* 68, no. 1, (1994): 9–14, http://www.questia.com.
21. Morrison, p. 45.
22. Ibid., p. 43.
23. Ibid., p. 45.
24. Ibid., p. 117.
25. Barbara Hill Rigney, *The Voices of Toni Morrison* (Columbus, OH: Ohio State University Press, 1991), p. 44.
26. Morrison, p. 182.
27. Philip M. Weinstein, *What Else But Love? The Ordeal of Race in Faulkner and Morrison* (New York: Columbia University Press, 1996), p. 156.
28. Christian, pp. 52–53.
29. Morrison, p. 5.
30. Ibid., p. 17.
31. John Leonard, "Books of the Times," *New York Times*, November 13, 1970, http://www.nytimes.com/books/98/01/11/home/morrison-bluest.html.
32. Morrison, p. 216.
33. Adam Langer, "Star Power: *Love* Is Toni Morrison's Best Novel in More than a Decade. Now She's Aiming Even Higher," *Book Magazine*, November–December 2003, 40, http://www.questia.com.
34. Wilfred D. Samuels and Clenora Hudson-Weems, *Toni Morrison* (Boston: Twayne Publishers, 1990), p. 6.
35. "Morrison's 'Bluest Eye' Joins Wide Range of Books Challenged in Alabama Schools," *School Library Journal*, September 2013, http://www.slj.com/2013/09/censorship/morrisons-bluest-eye-joins-wide-range-of-books-challenged-in-alabama-schools.

36. Colbert Report, "Toni Morrison," http://thecolbertreport. cc.com/videos/9yc4ry/toni-morrison (accessed July 29, 2015).

Chapter 5. Freedom Flight

1. Elissa Schappel, "Toni Morrison, The Art of Fiction No. 134," *Paris Review*, Fall 1993.
2. Ibid.
3. Wilfred D. Samuels and Clenora Hudson-Weems, *Toni Morrison* (Boston: Twayne Publishers, 1990), p. 6.
4. Barbara Christian, *Black Feminist Criticism: Perspectives on Black Women Writers* (New York: Teachers College Press, 1997), p. 61.
5. Toni Morrison, *Song of Solomon* (Plume: New York, 1987), p. 9.
6. Ibid., p. 180.
7. Trudier Harris, "Toni Morrison: Solo Flight Through Literature into History," *World Literature Today* 68, no. 1, (1994): 9–14, http://www.questia.com.
8. Morrison, pp. 10–11.
9. Ibid., p. 11.
10. Robert Sargent, "26 Ways of Ordering Experience: A Study of Toni Morrison's *The Bluest Eye* and *Sula*," *Faith of a Woman Writer*, eds. Alice Kessler-Harris and William McBrien (New York: Greenwood Press, 1988), p. 230.
11. Christian, p. 55.
12. Sargent, p. 231.
13. Harris.
14. Patrick Bryce Bjork, *The Novels of Toni Morrison: The Search for Self and Place within the Community* (New York: Peter Lang, 1996), p. 84.

Chapter 6. More Than a Ghost Tale

1. Toni Morrison, "A Bench by the Road." *Unitarian Universalist World*, Jan.–Feb. 1989, http://www.uuworld.org/articles/a-bench-by-road.

2. Trudier Harris, "Toni Morrison: Solo Flight Through Literature into History," *World Literature Today* 68, no. 1, (1994): 9–14, http://www.questia.com.

3. "Stampede of Slaves. A Tale of Horror!" *Cincinnati Enquirer*, January 29, 1856, http://www.enquirer.com/editions/1998/10/02/loc_w_slave02.html.

4. The Toni Morrison Society, "Bench by the Road Project," http://www.tonimorrisonsociety.org/bench.html (accessed July 20, 2015).

5. Bonnie Angelo, "The Pain of Being Black," *Time*, May 22, 1989, http://www.time.com/time/community/pulitzerinterview.html.

6. Toni Morrison, *Beloved* (New York: Plume, 1988), p. 247.

7. Ibid., pp. 198–99.

8. Ibid., p. 219.

9. Ibid., p. 186.

10. Barbara Hill Rigney, *The Voices of Toni Morrison* (Columbus, OH: Ohio State University Press, 1991), p. 41.

11. Peter J. Capuano, "Truth in Timbre: Morrison's Extension of Slave Narrative Song in *Beloved*," *African American Review* 37, no. 1, (2003).

12. Romans 9:25 (New King James Version).

13. Morrison, p. 57.

14. Ibid., p. 66.

15. Ibid., p. 273.

16. Ibid., p. 165.

17. Ibid.

18. Wilfred D. Samuels and Clenora Hudson-Weems, *Toni Morrison* (Boston: Twayne Publishers, 1990), p. 134.
19. Morrison, p. 252.
20. Ibid., pp. 86–87.
21. Ibid., p. 87.
22. Ibid., p. 89.
23. Ibid., p. 184.
24. Rigney, pp. 40–41.
25. Morrison, p. 256.
26. Ibid.
27. Ibid.
28. Ibid.
29. Walter Clemons, "A Gravestone of Memories," *Newsweek*, September 28, 1997, 75.
30. Scott Galupo, "Screen Saviors; Good Movies Made from Bad Novels and Vice Versa," *Washington Times*, October 17, 2003, http://www.questia.com.
31. Adam Langer, "*Love* Is Toni Morrison's Best Novel in More than a Decade. Now She's Aiming Even Higher," *Book Magazine*, November–December 2003, http://www.questia.com.

Chapter 7. The Dancing Mind

1. John Young, "Toni Morrison, Oprah Winfrey, and Postmodern Popular Audiences," *African American Review* 35, no. 2, (2001), http://www.questia.com.
2. Kara Walker, "Toni Morrison's 'God Help the Child'" *New York Times*, April 13, 2015, http://www.nytimes.com/2015/04/19/books/review/toni-morrisons-god-help-the-child.html

3. Toni Morrison and Slade Morrison, *Who's Got Game? Poppy or The Snake?* (New York: Scribner, 2003), interior cover flap.

4. Dinita Smith, "Toni Morrison's Mix of Tragedy, Domesticity, and Folklore," *New York Times*, January 8, 1998.

5. Trudier Harris, "Toni Morrison: Solo Flight Through Literature into History," *World Literature Today* 68, no. 1, (1994): 9–14, http://www.questia.com.

6. Ed Bradley, "Justice, Delayed but Not Denied," *CBS News: 60 Minutes*, October 21, 2004, http://www.cbsnews.com/stories/2004/10/21/60minutes/main650652.shtml.

7. Joseph C. Phillips, "Standing on Anonymous Shoulders," *Lee Bailey's EURWeb*, http://www.eurweb.com/story.cfm?id=18577 (accessed May 16, 2005).

8. Bradley.

9. The Toni Morrison Society, "Bench by the Road Project," http://www.tonimorrisonsociety.org/bench.html (accessed July 20, 2015).

10. Wilfred D. Samuels and Clenora Hudson-Weems, *Toni Morrison* (Boston: Twayne Publishers, 1990), p. 142.

11. Ann Geracimos, "Writer Toni Morrison through the Eyes of Friends: Always a Champion of Language," *Washington Times*, March 24, 1966, 3, http://www.questia.com.

Literary Terms

ambiguity—The quality of being obscure, in doubt, or uncertain.

antithesis—The exact opposite.

epitome—The best example of a characteristic of something.

genre—A class of literary works that usually shares a common content or style.

irony—A literary device that usually expresses the opposite, rather than the actual or literal meaning, of a word or phrase.

metaphor—A literary device in which one thing is said to be another. *Example: John was a raging bull in the wrestling match.*

protagonist—A main character of a novel, drama, or other literary work.

pseudonym—A fictitious name by which a writer chooses to be known; a pen name.

stereotype—A standard used to define a thing, idea, image, or opinion in an oversimplified or prejudicial manner.

symbolism—A literary device that uses a person or thing to represent someone or something else.

thesis—A thorough written analysis of a specific subject that students in graduate school must complete.

Major Works by Toni Morrison

Novels

The Bluest Eye
Sula
Song of Solomon
Tar Baby
Beloved
Jazz
Paradise
Love
A Mercy
Home
God Help the Child

Children's Books (*coauthored with son Slade Morrison):

*The Big Box**
*Who's Got Game? series**
Remember: The Journey to School Integration
*Peeny Butter Fudge**
*Little Cloud and Lady Wind**
*Please, Louise**

Other Projects (including works edited):

Dreaming Emmett (play)
Playing in the Dark: Whiteness and the Literary Imagination
Race-ing Justice, En-gendering Power
The Dancing Mind
What Moves at the Margin: Selected Nonfiction
Desdemona (play)

FURTHER READING

Bloom, Harold, ed. *Toni Morrison*. Broomall, PA: Chelsea House, 2004.

Bryfonski, Dedria. *Slavery in Toni Morrison's Beloved*. San Diego: Greenhaven, 2012.

Graham, Amy Graham. *Celebrated African-American Novelists*. Berkeley Heights, NJ: Enslow, 2013.

Hinds, Maureen J. *How to Analyze the Works of Toni Morrison*. Edina, MN: ABDO, 2012.

Kramer, Barbara. *Toni Morrison: A Biography of a Nobel Prize-Winning Writer*. Berkeley Heights, N.J.: Enslow, 2013.

Websites

The Toni Morrison Society

www.tonimorrisonsociety.org/

Collection of critiques, scholarly publications, and projects focused on Toni Morrison's works.

The Toni Morrison Society Bench by the Road Project

www.tonimorrisonsociety.org/bench.html

History, locations, and photos regarding the commemorative bench project.

Nobel Prize.org—Toni Morrison's Acceptance Speech

http://www.nobelprize.org/nobel_prizes/literature/laureates/1993/morrison-lecture.html

Transcript of Toni Morrison's Nobel Prize acceptance speech.

INDEX

A

Austen, Jane, 39

B

Bard College, 42

Beloved
  character development,
    108, 110–115, 117–118
  feature film, 120
  literary devices, 13, 14–
    15, 103, 105–106, 117
  narrative style, 17
  plot development,
    106-108
  Pulitzer Prize for
    Fiction, 95
  reviews, 118–119
  themes, 24–25, 30–31, 98,
    100–101
  use of songs, 105
"Bench by the Road" Project,
  97, 125, 129
Bluest Eye, The, 9, 41, 42
  banned book, 75
  character development,
    55, 65–69
  idea for book, 56
  literary devices, 9, 55,
    69–71, 73
  lyricism, 17
  narrative style, 17, 62

  Oprah's Book Club
    selection, 73
  plot development, 62–64
  reviews, 73
  setting, 50
  structure, 61–62
  themes, 32, 58–59, 60
Bontemps, Arna, 10
Book-of-the-Month Club, 93
Brown University, 46

C

Chicago Tribune, 73
Christian, Barbara, 18, 33, 56,
  70, 90
Cincinnati Enquirer, 95
Civil War, 48, 50, 98
Clinton, Bill, 46
Columbia University, 46
Cornell University, 41

D

Dartmouth College, 46
Desdemona, 123
Detroit Opera House, 125
Dick and Jane series, 61, 69-
  70, 73
Dreaming Emmett, 123, 126

E

Emancipation
  Proclamation, 98

F

Faulkner, William, 48
Flaubert, Gustave, 39

G

Garner, Margaret, 95, 98,
    103, 125
Gates, Henry Louis, Jr., 34
Georgetown University, 46
Ghansah, Rachel Kaadzi, 21
God Help the Children,
    122–123
Great Depression, 10, 38, 62

H

Harlem Renaissance, 10, 38
Harris, Trudier, 20, 24, 44,
    47-48, 50, 64, 85, 92, 125
Harvard University, 46
Heinze, Denise, 21
Hemispheres magazine, 37
Howard University, 39, 41
Howard University
    Players, 39
Hughes, Langston, 10
Hurston, Zora Neale, 10, 56

J

Jazz, 123
    narrative style, 17
Johnson, James Weldon, 10

L

Lauret, Maria, 34
Li, Stephanie, 21, 23, 27

Lincoln, Abraham, 98
literary devices
    ambiguity, 11, 13, 31
    call-and-response, 11,
        14–15
    irony, 11, 13, 26, 69,
        88–89, 117
    symbolism, 11, 13, 26, 69,
        88–90, 92, 103, 105–106
Lorain High School, 39
Lorain, Ohio, 37, 129
Love, 123

M

McKay, Claude, 10
Morrison, Harold
    (husband), 41
    honorary degrees, 46
Morrison, Harold Ford
    (son), 41
Morrison, Slade Kevin (son),
    41, 45
Morrison, Toni
    and African-American
        culture, 23, 24, 33, 38
    awards, 7, 9, 42, 44, 46,
        77, 118, 125
    birth name Chloe
        Anthony, 37, 39
    birthplace, 37
    children, 41
    children's books, 123, 125
    critics, 34

early favorite authors, 39
early life, 37–39
editorial jobs, 41, 125
education, 38–39, 41
family influence, 38, 48
impact on African-
    American
    literature, 125
legacy, 125, 129
lyricism, 15
marriage, 41
memorable characters,
    18–19
Nobel Prize for Literature,
    9, 44
Presidential Medal of
    Freedom, 7
recent works,
    122–123, 125
teaching jobs, 41, 42
writing schedule, 47

N
Newsweek, 73
New York City, 42, 47, 93
New York State, 41
New York Times, 9, 73, 119,
    122, 125
Nobel Prize for Literature, 9,
    44, 48

O
Obama, Barack, 7

Ohio, 37, 129
Oprah's Book Club, 73, 120

P
Paradise, 34, 42, 122, 123
    themes, 31–32
Paris Review, 77
Presidential Medal of
    Freedom, 7
Princeton University, 42, 122
Pulitzer Prize for Fiction, 95

R
Random House, 41, 125
Rigney, Barbara Hill, 15, 33,
    67, 103, 115

S
Sara Lawrence College, 46
60 Minutes, 127
slavery, 24–25, 50, 94, 95, 97,
    98, 100–101, 115
Song of Solomon
    ambiguous ending, 82
    character development,
        82–88
    language, 79
    literary devices, 13–14,
        88–90, 92
    narrative style, 77
    plot development, 80–82
    reviews, 77, 93
    structure, 79
    theater adaptation, 93

themes, 25, 27, 29–30, 32, 77, 79
Southern settings, 48, 50
State University of New York at Albany, 42
Sula, 19, 42, 56
  themes, 29

T

Tar Baby, 19, 42
Temple, Shirley, 58, 59
Texas Southern University, 41
"The Colbert Report," 73
themes, 21
  community and cultural issues, 11, 101–103
  personal identity, 11, 25, 27, 29, 77
  race relations, 11, 24, 47, 58–60
  relationships, 11, 29–30, 32
  sexuality, 11, 32-33
  slavery, 11, 98, 100–103
  spirituality/supernatural, 11, 30–32
Till, Emmett, 85, 123, 126-127
Tolstoy, 39
Toni Morrison Society, 97, 129

U

Underground Railroad, 115
University of Pennsylvania, 46
US Justice Department, 127

W

Walker, Kara, 122
Willis, Solomon (grandfather), 77
Winfrey, Oprah, 73, 120
Wofford, George (father), 37
Wofford, Ramah (mother), 37, 38
Woolf, Virginia, 48

Y

Yale University, 42, 46